# Developing
Self-Control

# Developing Self-Control

## Carol Foster

Bureau of Child Research
Camelot Behavioral Systems
Parsons, Kansas

F. FOURNIES & ASSOCIATES, INC.
129 Edgewood Drive
Bridgewater, N.J. 08807
(201) 526-2442

*OTHER BOOKS FROM F. FOURNIES & ASSOCIATES, INC.*

**Coaching for Improved Work Performance**
**Management Performance Appraisal – A National Study**
**Salesman Performance Appraisal – A National Study**

ISBN: 0-917472-02-0 (previously ISBN: 0-914-47412-X)

**Printer:** Edwards Brothers, Inc.
2500 South State Street
Ann Arbor, Michigan 48104

**Copyright** © **1974** by F. Fournies & Associates, Inc., 129 Edgewood Drive, Bridgewater, N.J. 08807. This book may not be reproduced in any form or by any means, except for the inclusion of brief quotations in a review, without permission from F. Fournies & Associates, Inc.

**First Printing: July, 1974**
**Second Printing: June, 1975**
**Third Printing: August, 1980**

# Contents

|  | Page |
|---|---|
| Introduction | vii |
| **Section 1: Changing Behavior** | 3 |
|     Chapter 1: Positive Reinforcement | 5 |
|     Chapter 2: Extinction | 17 |
|     Chapter 3: Observable Behavior | 25 |
| Self-Test | 35 |
| **Section 2: Measuring Behavior Change** | 39 |
|     Chapter 4: Baseline | 41 |
|     Chapter 5: Cumulative Graphs | 49 |
|     Chapter 6: Setting Goals | 69 |
| Self-Test | 90 |
| **Section 3: Maintaining Behavior Change** | 95 |
|     Chapter 7: Integrating Extinction and Punishment into Self-Control Programs | 97 |
|     Chapter 8: Establishing Maintenance Programs | 113 |
| Self-Test | 121 |
| Conclusion | 128 |
| Appendix | 133 |
| Bibliography | 134 |
| Validation | 136 |

Carol "Sunny" Foster is currently the director of program development at Project MORE (Mediated Operational Research in Education) where she is involved in program development and evaluation, staff training, and accountability. She is also on the staff of Camelot Behavioral Systems, which she helped to organize. In addition, she has served as director of in-service training at the State Home and Training School in Pueblo, Colorado, director of training at North Aurora Center in Illinois, and research director at University College, Southern Methodist University.

Her duties have included extensive program development for both staff and residents in the areas of accountability, training, and behavior modification. Ms. Foster brings her expertise in the field to this book, **Developing Self-Control.**

# Introduction

The purpose of this book is to assist you in understanding and changing your own behavior. Its format is probably unfamiliar and perhaps strange to most readers, but it is arranged according to the same behavioral principles that the text is designed to teach. It requires an answer to every numbered item, or **Frame.** The author's answers are written directly below each question. While your responses do not have to be identical to the author's, they should be similar in meaning. You should complete your response to each frame and then check it with the author's. If there is any error or uncertainty, you can immediately review and clear up any misunderstanding before proceeding.

The information and the questions for each frame are on a white background, the answers are in the shaded area. To use the book, cover all but the white part of the top frame on the page. Write your answers on a separate sheet of paper, uncover the answers (the grey area) for that frame, and compare your answers, then proceed to the next frame.

In addition to learning to recognize, understand, and use the principles of behavior involved in self-control, you will have a chance to apply them in your own self-control program. As you go through this book you will be taking data on your performance (for example, the time you spend answering the frames, the number of questions that you correctly answer, etc.). These data can be used for practice in the various self-control procedures that you will learn as you progress through this book. On page 131 you will find a sample data sheet. Use this as a model for your own record.

Begin taking data when you start Frame 1. Write down the date and the time you start. When you stop, record that time as well as the total time you have spent. You will also want to record the number of frames that you have completed correctly during that period. When you start working in the book again, even if it's the same day, start another line and keep the same data. Continue taking data in this manner throughout the book.

Periodic Self-Tests will help you in evaluating which chapters, if any, you should review. The Self-Test at the end of Section 3 covers the entire book. If you can successfully answer all of the items on this test you should have enough information to manage your own behavior! Enjoy your new control and remember — **THROUGH SELF-CONTROL, ONE CAN TRULY ACHIEVE FREEDOM.**

Section **1**

# Changing Behavior

This book has been written to help individuals manage their own behavior by controlling the consequences of that behavior. While specific examples of "behaviors" will be used, remember, the principles governing them can be used to manage any response if it meets the following criteria:

1. The behavior has to be measurable. That is, you must be able to count the number of times that the behavior occurs (e.g., the number of math problems accomplished), or the duration of the response (e.g., the length of crying time before a child falls asleep).
2. You must be able to control the consequences of the behavior. Behaviors that you want to increase must be followed by pleasant consequences.

The first section of the book has the following instructional goals:

Chapter 1: When you have finished this chapter you will be able to define and identify a positive reinforcer.
Chapter 2: When you have finished this chapter you will be able to define and identify the procedure of extinction.
Chapter 3: When you have finished this chapter you will be able to identify and deal with measurable behaviors.

# 1
Positive Reinforcement

In order to change the rate of a behavior, you have to control the consequences of that behavior. Essentially, responses can have three kinds of consequences: pleasant, unpleasant, or neutral. These can occur either singly or in combination.

If you examine a behavior that occurs frequently (at a high rate) you will discover that it usually has a pleasant consequence following it.

Behaviors that occur at low rates generally have either unpleasant consequences or neutral consequences following them, and the behaviors are not pleasant themselves. For instance, doing algebra problems is a low-rate behavior for many people: the behavior itself is generally unpleasant, and there are no immediate pleasant consequences following the response.

Other behaviors like watching a movie are in themselves pleasant experiences and therefore reinforcing. Still others, like taking a driver's test, are unpleasant, but are followed by the pleasant consequence of being able to drive legally.

**1**  A. What kinds of consequences would you use following a response that you wanted to increase in rate?

B. What kinds of consequences would you use following a response that you wanted to decrease in rate?

---

A. Pleasant ones.

B. Unpleasant ones (and/or neutral ones).

**2** In learning to control behaviors, there are certain behavioral principles that you will have to learn. They will be introduced in the program, but they are also listed in the appendix. Refer to them as you need to.

The First Behavioral Principle is: **Positive Reinforcement. Responses that are followed by a positive reinforcer will increase in rate.**

A. How can you get a response to increase in rate?

> A. Follow the response with a positive reinforcer.

**3** A positive reinforcer has two characteristics:

1. The positive reinforcer **follows** the response, and
2. The positive reinforcer **increases the rate** of that response.

Both of these characteristics are always present. If one of them is missing then you don't have a positive reinforcer.

A. Can an object be a positive reinforcer for a response if it comes before that response?
B. Can an object be a positive reinforcer for a response if it does not increase the rate of that response?

> A. No.
>
> B. No.

Positive Reinforcement

**4** A. What are the two characteristics that a positive reinforcer must have?

> A. It must follow the response and increase the rate of that response.

**5** Sandy's rate of brushing her teeth increased when tooth-brushing was followed by playing outside.

   A. What is the response being reinforced?
   B. What is the positive reinforcer?
   C. How do you know that the event was a positive reinforcer?

> A. Tooth-brushing.
>
> B. Playing outside.
>
> C. The response increased in rate when followed by the event.

**6** A. According to the First Behavioral Principle, if candy is a positive reinforcer for Susie, and you give Susie candy every time she hangs up her coat without being told to, what will happen to her rate of hanging up her coat?

> A. That rate will increase.

**7** A. True or false? The definition of a positive reinforcer is: a positive reinforcer is a reward for being good.

> A. False. A positive reinforcer has to follow the response and increase the rate of that response.

**8** Reading science fiction is a positive reinforcer for Sterno.

  A. How would you increase Sterno's rate of doing arithmetic problems?

> A. You would let him read science fiction after he has finished his arithmetic.

**9** A. If you want to increase the rate of a response, you _____ that response.

> A. Reinforce.

**10** An object or an event which follows a response and increases the rate of that response is a positive reinforcer.

Mrs. Franchetta gives Timmy candy every time he yells so that he'll be quiet. Timmy yells at a high rate.

  A. What response is Mrs. Franchetta reinforcing?
  B. What is the positive reinforcer?

> A. Yelling.

Positive Reinforcement

> B. Candy.

**11** There are two requirements that an object or event must fulfill before it is considered a positive reinforcer.

    1.    It **must follow** the response.
    2.    It **must increase the rate** of that response.

  A.  If Sally decides that she will play one more game of bridge before she goes to study, is it possible that this particular game of bridge will reinforce studying?
  B.  Justify your answer?

> A. No.
>
> B. It would have to follow the response, and this game of bridge comes before the response (studying).

**12** A.  What two requirements must be met for an object or an event to qualify as a positive reinforcer?

> A.  1.  It must follow the response.
>
>      2.  It must increase the rate of that response.

**13** A.  Responses that are followed by a _____ increase in rate.

B. If no reinforcer follows studying behavior, will the rate of studying increase?

> A. Positive reinforcer (or, reinforcer).
>
> B. No.

**14** Knowledge of results (e.g., the grade on a test) acts as a positive reinforcer for many people.

A. Are the results available in this program?

> A. Yes, by comparing your answers to those of the author.

**15** In this program, the correct answers follow each frame. For most students, if there is a high error rate on a program (that is, if they miss many items), they don't continue in the program because they are not positively reinforced. If they have a low error rate, then answering the frames is positively reinforced, and it increases in rate. Knowing the results is frequently a positive reinforcer if the student responds correctly.

A. In this program, what response is being positively reinforced by your being able to check the results?
B. Does the reinforcer follow the correct response?
C. Should the response rate of answering the questions increase?

> A. Answering the frames correctly is the response being reinforced.

Positive Reinforcement        11

> B. Yes, if you follow the program as designed: first, answer the question, then check the author's answer.
>
> C. Yes. Most people have over 90% of the items correct on this program. And most of those who start the program complete it.

**16** Sleep is a positive reinforcer for Jeff.

A. If Jeff sleeps after he has read twenty pages of **Developing Self-Control** what will happen to his rate of reading this book?

> A. It will increase in rate.

**17** In the following examples, identify which object or event, because of sequence, could be a possible positive reinforcer, and what response will increase in rate if it is:

A. José reads science fiction and then does math problems.
Possible positive reinforcer: _____
Response: _____

B. King Lear has an ice cream cone after he cleans house.
Possible positive reinforcer: _____
Response: _____

C. Mrs. Nixon gives Mr. Nixon five dollars after he finishes watching a football game on television so that he will cut the grass.
Possible positive reinforcer: _____
Response: _____

D. Lady Godiva writes a letter to her boyfriend after doing dishes.
Possible positive reinforcer: _____
Response: _____

---

A. Doing math problems.
Reading science fiction.

B. Ice cream cone.
Cleaning house.

C. Five dollars.
Watching television. (The five dollars follows watching television, not mowing the lawn.)

D. Writing a letter.
Doing dishes.

---

**18** A. Define a positive reinforcer. (Remember that you must list two characteristics.) A positive reinforcer is an object or an event that _____.

---

A. Follows a response and increases the rate of that response.

---

Now, that you have completed Chapter 1, you should be able to define and identify a positive reinforcer. The use of positive reinforcement is one of the key procedures in arranging consequences for behavior. Since the basic idea in changing behavior is to arrange situations so that desirable behavior is reinforced and unwanted behavior is not reinforced, I highly recommend using this procedure in setting up your own behavior control programs.

Positive Reinforcement

If you answered Frame 18 correctly, take a break before starting Chapter 2. If you missed Frame 18, complete the following review before starting Chapter 2. Remember to continue taking data.

**Review of Positive Reinforcement**

**19** A. An object or an event is a positive reinforcer if it follows a response and _____ the rate of that response.

>A. Increases

**20** A. Can an object, or an event, be a positive reinforcer for ironing if it is presented before the ironing occurs.

>A. No. It must follow the response (ironing).

**21** A. What two characteristics must an object or an event have for it to be a positive reinforcer?

    1. It _____ a response.
    2. It _____ the rate of that response.

>A. 1. Follows
>    2. Increases

Changing Behavior

**22** A. A response that has been followed by a positive reinforcer will _____ in rate.

> A. Increase

**23** A. Elaine wants to increase her rate of sewing. If translating French is a positive reinforcer for her how can she increase her rate of sewing?
B. Margaret has a different problem: she doesn't get her French assignment done, but sewing is a positive reinforcer for her. How can she increase her rate of translating French?

> A. Elaine can translate French after she sews.
>
> B. Margaret can sew after she translates French.

**24** A. Define a positive reinforcer: A positive reinforcer is an object or an event that _____.

> A. Follows a response and increases the rate of that response.

If you answered Frame 24 correctly, take a break and then begin the next Chapter. If you missed it, review Chapter 1 before proceeding.

# 2
# Extinction

The Second Behavioral Principle is: **Extinction.**
**Responses which have previously been established or maintained by reinforcement will decrease in rate when that reinforcement is withheld.**

In other words, if you have been reinforcing a response and you stop presenting the reinforcer after that response, the response will occur less frequently.

**1** A. You have increased your rate of studying by listening to the stereo after completing your assignments. Your stereo breaks down, and you can no longer use it for a consequence for studying. What happens to your studying rate?

> A. Your rate of studying will decrease; your behavior of studying will extinguish.

**2** A. If knowing the test results is the positive reinforcer that has kept you responding this long in the present program, how could we extinguish this response?

> A. We could stop presenting the answers following each frame.

**3** A. If playing cards is a positive reinforcer for Bonnie's practicing the piano, how could she increase her rate of piano playing?

A. She could play cards after she practices the piano.

**4** A. How could Bonnie decrease the rate of piano playing once it had been increased?

A. She could stop following piano playing with card playing.

**5** A. If mother's attention is a positive reinforcer for Sam, and she gives him a lecture every time he swears, what will happen to the rate of Sam's swearing?

A. Sam's rate of swearing will increase because she is giving him a lecture, and therefore, her attention, after he swears.

**6** A. How could Sam's mother extinguish his swearing behavior?

A. She can stop reinforcing his swearing. Stop giving him attention when he swears.

**7** A. Extinction results in a decrease in the rate of a response. How is this reduction obtained?

A. By no longer reinforcing the response. By no longer following

# Extinction

the response with a reinforcer.

**8** A. The process of extinction is a decrease in the response rate that occurs _____.

A. When that response is no longer followed by a reinforcer.

**9** A. How can you tell if watching television is an effective positive reinforcer for Peter's feeding the dog?

A. Don't let Peter watch television until he has fed the dog and see if his rate of feeding the dog increases. (For this particular response, for obvious reasons, you will probably want to have a maximum number of times per day that he can feed the dog. For instance, feeding the dog at 8 A.M. would allow Peter to watch television, for a specific amount of time, until the next feeding.)

**10** Sarah Jane has been using talking on the telephone as a positive reinforcer for doing yoga exercises. She has increased her yoga exercising to a high rate. Because she forgot to pay her phone bill (probably because she spent so much time doing yoga exercises) her phone has been disconnected, and can no longer be used as a positive reinforcer.

    A. What will happen to her rate of exercising?
    B. What behavioral principle is in effect?

> A. That rate will decrease since it is no longer being followed by a positive reinforcer.
>
> B. Extinction. (Second Behavioral Principle)

**11** Until Sarah Jane gets her phone reconnected, she decides to try showering as the positive reinforcer for exercising.

  A. How will she know if it is a positive reinforcer?

> A. If taking a shower is a positive reinforcer for Sarah Jane's exercising and she takes a shower after her yoga exercises, then her rate of exercising will increase.

**12** A. What will happen to Sarah Jane's rate of yoga exercising if showering is not a reinforcer for exercising?

> A. That rate will continue to decrease.

**13** A. Define positive reinforcer.
B. State the principle of extinction.

> A. A positive reinforcer is an object or an event that follows a response and increases the rate of that response. (Did you have **both** parts of the definition?)

# Extinction

> B. Responses which have been previously established or maintained by reinforcement will decrease in rate when that reinforcement is withheld.

You should now be able to identify and define the procedure of extinction and the use of positive reinforcement. Extinction is quite useful in self-control procedures in that it is an effective way to eliminate undesirable behaviors from your repertoire. You can also use it to eliminate incompatible behaviors which compete with those desirable behaviors that you are trying to increase in rate. It is equally important, you will find, to be able to identify its occurrence in situations where you want to maintain or increase a behavior that is undergoing extinction. In Chapter 7 we will deal with this problem in more detail.

By the way, has your response of recording data extinguished?

---

If you answered the items in Frame 13 correctly, proceed to Chapter 3. Take a break if you want to. If you missed Part A, go back to Chapter 1 If you missed Part B, go through the following review.

**Review of Extinction**

**14** A. A response that has been followed by a positive reinforcer will increase in rate. Once that response has been increased, and if the reinforcer no longer follows that response, then that response rate will decrease. This process is called _____.

> A. Extinction.

**15** A. Riley has been using working in his garden to reinforce completing his statistics assignments. What predictions can you make about his rate of doing statistics assignments when winter comes and the snow falls?

B. What is the process called?

---

A. His rate of doing statistics assignments will decrease.

B. Extinction.

---

**16** A. When a response is followed by a positive reinforcer, you get (a decrease/an increase) in the rate of that response.
B. When the positive reinforcer no longer follows the response, then you get (a decrease/an increase) in the rate of that response.

---

A. An increase

B. A decrease

---

**17** A. How can you increase the rate of a response?
B. How can you decrease the rate of a response?

---

A. Reinforce that response. (Have a positive reinforcer follow the response.)

B. Extinguish that response. (Stop following the response with a reinforcer.)

Extinction

**18** A. State the principle of extinction.

> A. Responses which have been previously established or maintained by reinforcement will decrease in rate when that reinforcement is withheld.

If you answered Frame 18 correctly, proceed to Chapter 3. Review if you need to.

# 3
# Observable Behavior

Behaviors are reinforced by many different objects and events. These vary from person to person, and the same object or event may be a reinforcer at one time, and not at another. (For instance, an individual's behavior may not be reinforced by a steak dinner when he has the flu, whereas, two days later, the steak may be quite reinforcing.) Because we can't make a definite statement about what are always positive reinforcers, we have to establish definite criteria for identification. This chapter will show you how you can recognize them by their effects on behavior.

**1** For two years, Sam has been nagging his son to quit teasing his little sister. Sam's younger brother (who happens to be a psychologist) suggests that the nagging is a positive reinforcer for his son's teasing.

  A. What can Sam do to find out if nagging is a positive reinforcer for his son's teasing?

---

You should have either or both of the following answers:

A. 1. Sam can stop nagging his son about teasing and see if his rate of teasing decreases. (Extinction)

   2. He can nag his son after some other response and see if the rate of that response increases. (Positive reinforcement)

---

**2** The answers to the above questions seem straightforward, but there is a hang-up: How can Sam tell if the rate has decreased? Does this mean that his son has to stop teasing completely? What must his rate of teasing be in order for Sam to come to the conclusion that his nagging is a positive reinforcer for the boy's teasing?

A. If Sam's son teased his sister 45 minutes a day before Sam started the extinction procedure, and he teased his sister 5 minutes a day when Sam no longer nagged, could you conclude that nagging is a positive reinforcer for the teasing?

B. If the rate of teasing before the extinction procedure began was 45 minutes a day and the rate afterward was three hours a day, could you conclude that nagging is a positive reinforcer for his son's teasing?

A. Yes, the response rate decreased considerably (from 45 minutes to 5 minutes) when the response was no longer followed by nagging.

B. No, the response rate did not decrease. In fact, there was a large increase, so you could not conclude that nagging was the positive reinforcer.

**3** A. The above frame demonstrates that there are two criteria for determining if an event is a positive reinforcer. The first is the rate of the response before you start your procedure ( of extinction or of positive reinforcement) and the other is _____.

A. The rate of the response after your procedure is begun.

Observable Behavior

**4** Juanita enjoys training horses and wonders if that might be a positive reinforcer for a particular behavior. She wants to increase the amount of time she spends as a volunteer at the hospital. She currently works six hours a week at the hospital.

    A. What is her response rate before beginning the reinforcement procedure?
    B. How will she know if training horses is a positive reinforcer for her volunteer work?

> A. Six hours a week.
>
> B. If there is an increase in her volunteer hours when she uses training horses as a positive reinforcer for volunteer work.

**5** The two ways to determine if an object or an event is a positive reinforcer are:

    A. Present the object or event after some response. This will result in a(n) _____ in the rate of that response if the object or event is a positive reinforcer.
    B. Stop presenting the object or event after the specified response. This will result in a(n) _____ in the rate of that response if the object or event is a positive reinforcer.

> A. Increase
>
> B. Decrease

**6** How can you determine if an object or event is a positive reinforcer?

A. _____
B. _____

---

A. Stop presenting the object or event after some response which it has followed in the past. If the rate of that response decreases, then it was a positive reinforcer.

B. Present the object or event after some other response. If the rate of that response increases, then it was a positive reinforcer.

---

**7** There is a way to **guess** what may be reinforcing to an individual. If he or she spends a lot of time engaged in some behavior, then it is **probably** a reinforcer.

A. If an individual spends a lot of time smoking cigarettes, is cigarette smoking probably a reinforcer?

---

A. Yes.

---

**8** A. What is a good way to guess what may be reinforcing to an individual?

---

A. Observe his or her activities. (Observe how one spends his or her time.)

---

**9** Charlie does each of the following things each day:

1. Drinks coffee (three hours)
2. Reads novels (two hours)
3. Irons (15 minutes)

A. Which of these activities would you guess is the most reinforcing to him?

---

A. Drinking coffee

---

**10** A. How would you **know** if coffee drinking has been the positive reinforcer for Charlie's sitting down at the kitchen table?

---

A. Don't let him drink coffee when he sits down and see if his rate of sitting down decreases. If it decreases then it is probably a reinforcer for that response.

---

**11** Another way to find out if coffee is positively reinforcing to Charlie is to have it follow some other response and see if it increases the rate of that response. Charlie currently reads 15 pages of physics a day, and he would like to increase that rate.

A. How could he find out if coffee drinking is a positive reinforcer for his reading physics?

---

A. Let him drink coffee after reading physics. If his rate increases (to more than 15 pages per day) then drinking coffee is a positive reinforcer for Charlie's reading.

**12** A. What are the two ways to **know** if an event is a positive reinforcer?

> A. 1. Have the event follow some specified response and see if the rate of that response increases.
>
> 2. Stop following the response with a particular event and see if the rate of that response decreases.

**13** If a person spends a lot of time freely engaging in some behavior, that behavior is probably reinforcing.

A. How can you **guess** what is a positive reinforcer for yourself?

> A. Observe how you spend your free time. Those behaviors that occur most frequently are probable positive reinforcers.

**14** A. Once you have made a **guess** about what could be a positive reinforcer for your own behavior, how can you find out if it **actually** is a positive reinforcer?

> A. Have this event follow some response and see if that response increases in rate.
> or
> (Stop having this event follow some response that it has previously followed and see if that response decreases in rate.)

**15** Rudolph spends a lot of his free time watching birds.

A. Does this mean that bird watching is definitely reinforcing to Rudolph?

> A. No, it's probably a good guess, but you don't know for sure.

**16** A. How could Rudolph **know** for sure if bird watching is a reinforcer for him?

> A. Following some specified response, have him watch birds and see if the rate of that response increases.
> or
> (Try extinction.)

**17** Rudolph decides to see if bird watching will increase his rate of smiling at his wife. He smiles at her about once a day now. He decides that he'll watch birds only after he smiles at her five times a day. After just one weekend of this, he smiles at his wife 38 times a day.

A. Would you say that bird watching was a positive reinforcer for Rudolph's smiling at his wife?

> A. Yes.

**18** Rudolph happened to smile at his wife, Irene, while she was ironing. He noticed that her rate of ironing increased.

A. What can you assume about Rudolph's smile?

> A. His smile is a positive reinforcer for his wife's ironing.

**19** Rudolph decides that if he can accidentally increase the rate of his wife's ironing, he can increase other behaviors too. He decides that he will reinforce Irene's thinking pleasant thoughts about him by smiling at her when she does. He discusses this plan with Sam's brother, Ralph (the psychologist), who points out that Rudolph has no way of knowing if Irene is thinking about him. While Irene may know what she is thinking about Rudolph, there is no way for Rudolph himself to observe this type of behavior.
   A. If you don't know when the response is occurring, can you follow the response (consistently) with a positive reinforcer?

> A. No, you must be able to observe the behavior occurring in order to follow it with a positive reinforcer.

**20** Ralph and Rudolph discuss this and Rudolph comes up with a list of things he wants Irene to do more often:

   1. Smile
   2. Fix spaghetti
   3. Think more pleasant thoughts about him
   4. Read the sports page
   5. Cut the grass
   6. Develop a stronger superego

   A. Ralph looks over the list and tells Rudolph that four of the six are acceptable. Which four did he okay?

Observable Behavior 33

> A. Numbers 1, 2, 4, and 5 are readily observable. (For numbers 3 and 6, you might be able to come up with some observable responses which you might be able to justify as reflecting these concepts, but they themselves are not readily observable nor easily defined.)

**21** Rudolph decides to concentrate on increasing the rate of Irene's smiling.

A. How can he do this?

> A. Have him smile at her whenever she smiles at him.

In this chapter you have been introduced to three necessary skills for setting up your own self-control program: guessing what may be a positive reinforcer for a given behavior; determining if that object or event **is**, in fact, a positive reinforcer; and identifying which types of responses are defined in observable terms. You should now be able to come up with some ideas about what might be reinforcing to you. You should also begin to define some of your own behavior in observable terms.

After you have experienced some success with self-control programs, you will probably want to consider more difficult, less observable behaviors such as those that only you can see. For instance, you may be able to define and identify the behavior of self-critical thoughts. This is something that no one else can do for you. These behaviors are termed "covert" and are an extremely important part of self-control. While we don't cover this concept in the book, there are some excellent sources listed in the bibliography.

In order to evaluate whether or not you have acquired the critical skills from the last three chapters, take the Self-Test on the next page. If you make any mistakes, review the appropriate chapter before proceeding to Section 2.

# SECTION 1

## SELF-TEST

Count each of these questions as one frame for your data sheet.

**1** Define positive reinforcer.

**2** Define extinction.

**3** How do you know if an object or an event is a positive reinforcer?

**4** How can you guess what may be a positive reinforcer for an individual?

**5** Which of the following behaviors are more readily observable?
- a. Singing
- b. Crying
- c. Feeling sad
- d. Running
- e. Thinking about the weather
- f. Laughing
- g. Being upset
- h. Typing
- i. Swearing
- j. Getting only one cavity

**6** In each of the following examples, there are two events occurring. Only one of them could possibly act as the positive reinforcer. Identify this event in each example.
- a. Fred eats peanuts after he washes the dog.
- b. Ruthie does ten push-ups after reading fifty pages of Kant.
- c. Hubert does the dishes before going to the wrestling match.
- d. Sherry rides her horse before she mows the lawn.
- e. After taking a nap, Rudy plays with the dog.
- f. Delbert plays basketball and then gets drunk.

## ANSWERS

**1** A positive reinforcer is an object or an event that follows a response and increases the rate of that response.

**2** Responses which have been previously established or maintained by reinforcement will decrease in rate when that reinforcement is withheld.

**3** The two ways to know if an object or an event is a positive reinforcer are:

1. Have the object or event follow some response and see if the rate of that response increases.
2. Stop following a response with a particular event or object (which it has previously been following) and see if the rate of that response decreases.

**4** In order to guess what may be a positive reinforcer for an individual, observe how he spends his time. Those activities that he engages in most frequently, or at a high rate, are probable positive reinforcers.

**5** The following behaviors are more readily observable:

| | | | |
|---|---|---|---|
| a. | Singing | h. | Typing |
| b. | Crying | i. | Swearing |
| d. | Running | j. | Getting only one cavity |
| f. | Laughing | | |

**6** The following events could possibly act as positive reinforcers:

| | | | |
|---|---|---|---|
| a. | Eating peanuts | d. | Mowing the lawn |
| b. | Doing push-ups | e. | Playing with the dog |
| c. | Wrestling match | f. | Getting drunk |

Note: If you missed any part of No. 6, look back at the question and decide which event **follows** the other.

If you missed any of these Self-Test questions, review the appropriate Chapter.

# Section 2

# Measuring Behavior Change

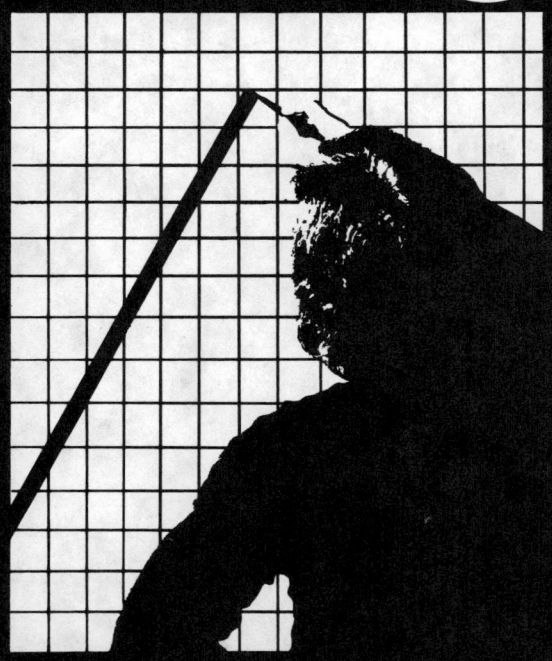

In Section 1 you saw how behavior is affected by its consequences — to change the rate of a response you must change the consequences of that response. You were also briefly introduced to the difference between observable external (overt) behaviors, and internal (covert) behaviors, which can't be directly observed and are, therefore, much more difficult to measure and arrange consequences for. This is extremely important since data gathering will be easier when you deal with observable events. And data gathering, of course, is crucial to any behavior change program. Data must be kept before intervention can even begin. And, it is essential that you keep data during any intervention phase of a self-control program.

The data gathered before intervention begins are called baseline data. These data should reflect the rate of the response before you make any attempts to alter that response. The baseline becomes the standard of comparison for any of the effects of your program. This section will cover the concept of baseline data and the ways in which you can use it in your own self-control program. You will also learn about the cumulative graph which provides an easy method for interpreting your data. In the final chapter of this section we'll discuss setting goals and their necessity and importance in any self-control program.

The second section of this book has the following instructional goals:

> Chapter 4: When you have finished this chapter you will be able to define and describe the use of baseline.
> Chapter 5: When you have finished this chapter you will be able to identify and correctly use a cumulative graph.
> Chapter 6: When you have finished this chapter you will be able to establish goals from baseline data.

# 4
# Baseline

**1**    A.    Define a positive reinforcer.

> A.    A positive reinforcer is an object or an event that follows a response and increases the rate of that response.

**2**    In order to determine if an event is a positive reinforcer, you have to know what the response rate was before positive reinforcement, or some other procedure was started. The rate of a response before any intervention procedure is begun is called a baseline.

      A.    Why should you obtain baseline data?

> A.    To see if some event is a positive reinforcer, you have to know the rate of the response before that event was used as a positive reinforcer.
> or
> To see if your self-control procedure was effective, you need to know the rate of the response before you began the self-control procedure.

**3**    A.    What is baseline?

> A.    Baseline is the rate of a response before you begin any intervention procedure.

**4** Jennifer took baseline data on her rate of translating German. She translated two and one-half pages a day during baseline. She is going to listen to the stereo for 30 minutes every time she translates two and one-half pages.

    A. How will she know if listening to the stereo is a positive reinforcer?

> A. After she has followed translating German with listening to her stereo, that rate will be above two and one-half pages a day if listening to the stereo is a positive reinforcer.

**5**   A. What information does a baseline provide?

> A. Baseline provides the rate of a response before any intervention procedure is begun.

**6**   A. Rocky read ten pages a week throughout the baseline period. During a self-control program he received cigarettes after reading a specified amount. He is now reading 200 pages a week. Are cigarettes a positive reinforcer for Rocky's reading?

> A. Yes.

**7**   A. Pearlie Mae read ten pages a week during baseline and ten pages a week during the self-control intervention phase when she received hot tea after reading a certain number of pages. Would you say that hot tea is a positive reinforcer for Pearlie Mae's reading?

> A. No. We can assume that tea is not a reinforcer for Pearlie Mae's reading, since her reading rate did not increase.

**8** A. If a student reads 30 pages a week during baseline and 20 pages per week during the self-control procedure phase, is her reading being reinforced?

> A. No.

**9** A. Can you tell if an event is a positive reinforcer without data?
B. How can you guess what is likely to be a positive reinforcer?

> A. No. You need data to know if an event is a positive reinforcer.
>
> B. Observe how someone spends his or her free time.

**10** Harvey reads 15 pages a week when we give him an apple after he reads.

A. Can you tell from this if apples are a positive reinforcer for Harvey's reading?
B. Justify your answer.

> A. No.

> B. You would need to know what his rate was before you gave him the apples for reading in order to know whether or not his rate of reading increased or decreased. The only way that an apple could be a positive reinforcer for his reading would be if his rate of reading increased.

**11** Clarence reads two pages per day. He decided that he would have a cup of coffee every time he sat down to study. After three weeks he still studied two pages a day. For the baseline period, Clarence sat down to study two times a day. During the third week of the self-control program, he sat down to study 15 times a day.

    A. What response was being followed by the cup of coffee?
    B. Was coffee a positive reinforcer for Clarence's sitting down?

> A. Sitting down.
>
> B. Yes, it increased his rate of sitting down from two times to 15 times a day.

**12**   A. What response would you reinforce so that Clarence's rate of reading would increase instead of his rate of sitting down?

> A. You would reinforce his reading of three or more pages instead of his merely sitting down.

**13**   A. How will you know if you have reinforced Clarence's reading?

# Baseline

> A. His rate of reading will increase above the baseline rate.

**14** A. Define baseline.
B. Why should you obtain baseline data?

> A. Baseline is the rate of a response before any intervention is begun.
>
> B. To see if the self-control procedure was successful; to see if some event is a positive reinforcer.

This chapter has covered the use of baseline data and its importance in any self-control program:

1. In determining if change is necessary
2. In determining the success of your program
3. In setting realistic goals

It is quite possible that after you collect baseline data on a particular behavior you may decide that the rate of the response is appropriate and it's not necessary for you to change it.

If you do decide to change a behavior, your baseline data becomes an essential gauge to measure your program data against. This comparison will show the success or failure of your attempts at change. Did the rate increase or decrease?

And finally, to simply institute and carry out a baseline phase you have to have a specific definition of the behavior. Establishing a baseline will give you a practical method for setting a realistic goal. This is essential in any self-modification program.

If you answered both parts of Frame 14 correctly, go on to Chapter 5. If you missed this last item, go through the following review. If you are planning to stop soon, this is a good place.

**Review of Baseline**

**15** A baseline is the measure of the rate of a response before you begin any intervention procedure. It should be used whenever you are planning to employ any method for changing the rate of a response; for instance, extinction.

   A.  Why would you get a baseline?

   A.  You would get a baseline in order to determine if a self-control procedure has had an effect on the rate of a response.

**16** Jessie reads 57 pages per day when she follows reading with playing with her children.

   A.  Is playing with her children reinforcing for Jessie?

   A.  There is no way to tell. You would need to know how many pages she'd read if she weren't using playing with her children as a consequence for reading. (In other words, you need a baseline.)

**17** Trini has to practice the piano three hours every day. She is currently practicing two hours per day.

Baseline

A. What is her rate of practice during baseline?

> A. Her rate during baseline is two hours a day.

**18** Trini decides to use playing softball as the positive reinforcer for practicing three hours a day.

A. How will she know if playing softball is a positive reinforcer for her practicing the piano?

> A. Her rate of practicing the piano will increase when she follows it with a game of softball.

**19** A. Why should you obtain a baseline?

> A. So you can tell if a procedure was successful.

**20** A. Define baseline.

> A. Baseline is the rate of a response before you begin any intervention procedure.

If you answered Frame 20 correctly, you have finished this chapter and can now take a break or proceed to the next chapter. If you missed the last item, please review this chapter.

# 5
# Cumulative Graphs

In order to draw conclusions from your data, it will help if you put the data on a graph. While there are several types of graphs we'll be using **Cumulative Graphs** in this book. We use these because it is easier to detect subtle changes in rates of responses on this type of graph.

When you use the cumulative graph you always add the previous responses to the current response frequency and plot that total. In other words, you accumulate your data. For example, if you have stroked your beard 4 times the first day, 3 times the second day, and 6 times the third day, you would graph the following data:

**1**
1.   4 (Day 1)
2.   7 (Day 1 + Day 2)
3.   13 (Day 1 + Day 2 + Day 3)

A.   What number would you graph if you stroked your beard 10 times on Day 4?

A.   23 (Day 1 + Day 2 + Day 3 + Day 4)

**2**   A.   What characteristic gives the cumulative graph its name?

A.   You always add (or accumulate) current responses to the previous ones and plot that number.

**3** Look at the graph below:

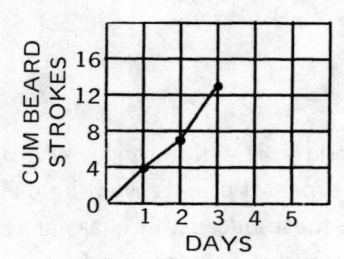

A. The horizontal line (the abscissa) is a measure of time, in this case, _____. (i.e., how is time measured?)
B. The vertical line (the ordinate) is a measure of the frequency of some response, in this case, _____.

> A. Days.
>
> B. Beard strokes (cumulative).

**4** A. What does the horizontal line usually indicate?
B. What does the vertical line indicate?

> A. Time (the passage of time).
>
> B. The cumulative number of some response.

**5** There are two steps in making a cumulative graph:

1. Accumulate your data.
2. Graph this cumulative data.

Cumulative Graphs

Let's go through Step 1 for the following data on Mr. Bluster's frowns. On the first day, he frowned 15 times. He frowned 12 times on the second day; 17 times on the third day; 14 times on the fourth day; and 17 times on the fifth day.

A.  Complete this chart.

|        | Number of Frowns | Cumulative Number of Frowns |
|--------|------------------|-----------------------------|
| Day 1  | 15               | 15                          |
| Day 2  | 12               | 27                          |
| Day 3  | 17               | ___                         |
| Day 4  | ___              | ___                         |
| Day 5  | ___              | 75                          |

A.  Your chart should look like this:

|        | Number of Frowns | Cumulative Number of Frowns |
|--------|------------------|-----------------------------|
| Day 1  | 15               | 15                          |
| Day 2  | 12               | 27                          |
| Day 3  | 17               | 44                          |
| Day 4  | 14               | 58                          |
| Day 5  | 17               | 75                          |

**6** A.  Which column in the above chart are you going to graph?

A.  The column labeled **Cumulative Number of Frowns.**

**7** The second step is to graph the cumulative number. The first two numbers are done.

A.  Complete the graph.

A. Your completed graph should look like this:

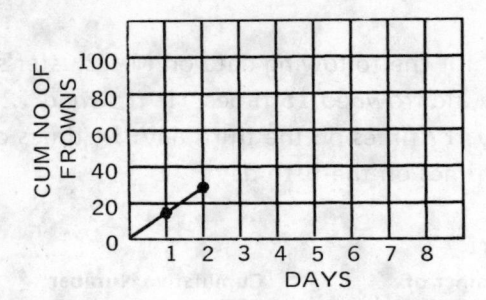

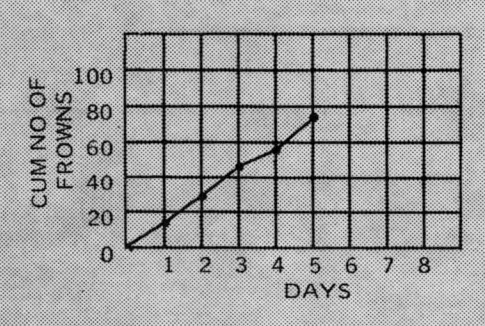

**8** Let's try another graph for practice. Remember to do both steps. Dave finds that he is always making promises that he knows he can't possibly keep, so he decides to get baseline data on the number of promises he doesn't keep.

A. Complete the chart.

|  | Number of Unkept Promises | Cumulative Number of Unkept Promises |
|---|---|---|
| Day 1 | 4 | 4 |
| Day 2 | 5 | 9 |
| Day 3 | 0 | 9 |
| Day 4 | 3 | — |
| Day 5 | 6 | — |
| Day 6 | 0 | — |
| Day 7 | 2 | — |

# Cumulative Graphs

B. Fill in the graph.

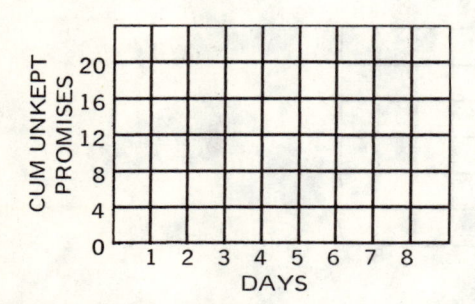

A.

| | Number of Unkept Promises | Cumulative Number of Unkept Promises |
|---|---|---|
| Day 1 | 4 | 4 |
| Day 2 | 5 | 9 |
| Day 3 | 0 | 9 |
| Day 4 | 3 | 12 |
| Day 5 | 6 | 18 |
| Day 6 | 0 | 18 |
| Day 7 | 2 | 20 |

B.

**9** There is one more aspect of a cumulative graph that you should know about. If you maintain your graph for a long enough period of time you will reach the top number of the graph, and have to start from the bottom again. This is called a **reset**. An example is given in the graph below:

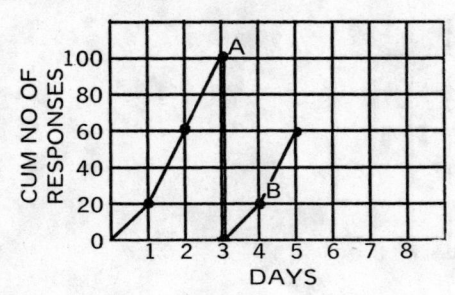

A. When does a reset occur?
B. What is the cumulative number of pages read at Point A?
C. What is the cumulative number of pages read at Point B?

---

A. When the line reaches the top of the graph, (i.e., when the accumulated figures reach the top of the graph).

B. 100 pages.

C. 120 pages.

---

**10** A. Cassandra is an astrologer, and she decided that she could design more charts a day if she followed her work with a positive reinforcer. Graph the data. Remember to make a reset.

|  | Number of Astrological Charts | Cumulative Number of Astrological Charts |
|---|---|---|
| Day 1 | 1 | — |
| Day 2 | 3 | — |
| Day 3 | 4 | — |
| Day 4 | 2 | — |
| Day 5 | 1 | — |
| Day 6 | 5 | — |

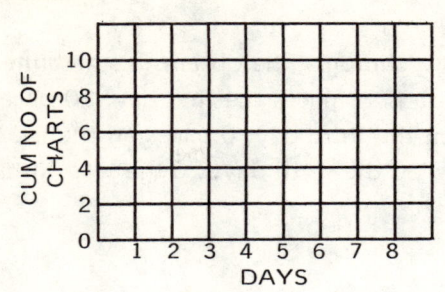

Cumulative Graphs

A.

|  | Number of Astrological Charts | Cumulative Number of Astrological Charts |
|---|---|---|
| Day 1 | 1 | 1 |
| Day 2 | 3 | 4 |
| Day 3 | 4 | 8 |
| Day 4 | 2 | 10 |
| Day 5 | 1 | 11 |
| Day 6 | 5 | 16 |

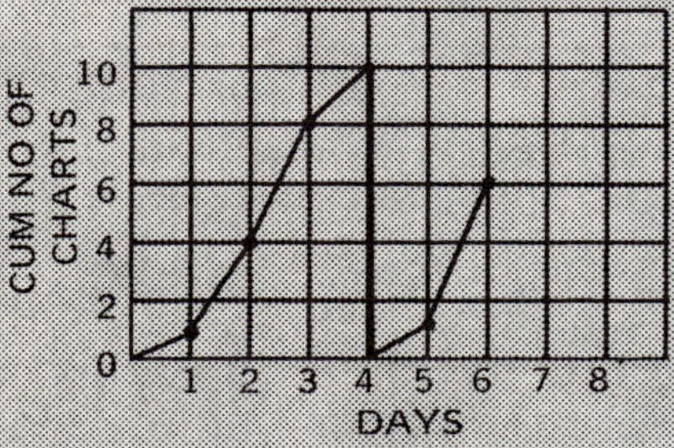

**11** A. Why should you get a baseline?

A. You should get a baseline so you can tell if the self-control program was successful.

**12** Clancy needs to increase the amount of time he spends reading his philosophy. Being a good psychologist, he obtains his baseline data of pages read per day. He reads 10 pages the first day, 20 pages on the second day, 15 pages on the third day, 0 pages on the fourth day, 15 pages the fifth day, 20 the sixth day, 20 the seventh day, and 10 the eigth day.

A. Construct your chart.
B. Fill in the graph.

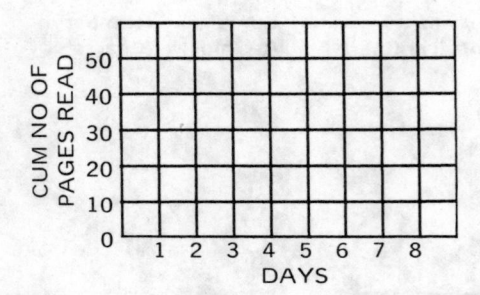

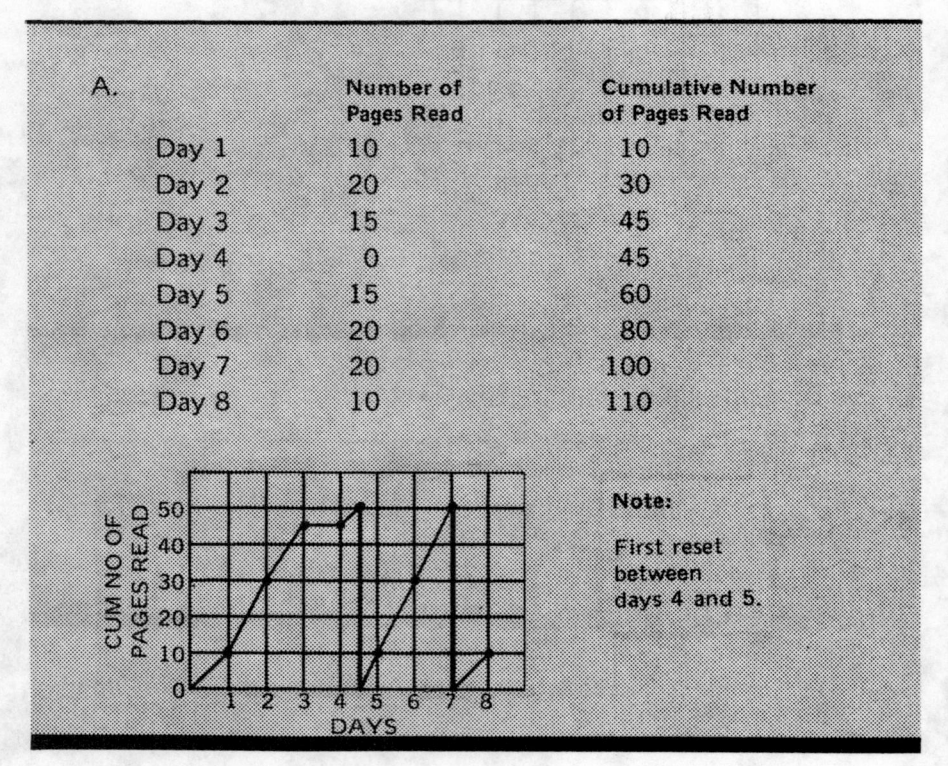

---

A.

| | Number of Pages Read | Cumulative Number of Pages Read |
|---|---|---|
| Day 1 | 10 | 10 |
| Day 2 | 20 | 30 |
| Day 3 | 15 | 45 |
| Day 4 | 0 | 45 |
| Day 5 | 15 | 60 |
| Day 6 | 20 | 80 |
| Day 7 | 20 | 100 |
| Day 8 | 10 | 110 |

Note:

First reset between days 4 and 5.

# Cumulative Graphs

The cumulative graph in this chapter was introduced to help you evaluate the success of your self-control program on a frequent and efficient basis. You should construct and use one of these graphs with **every** self-control program. You can greatly increase your ability to draw conclusions about the effectiveness of your program if you can see the data in the form of a graph. You may find that after several self-control programs the event of graphing the rate of the response you are controlling will act as a reinforcer for the behavior you are trying to modify.

While this chapter described "resets", I recommend that, when constructing a graph, you estimate how many responses will be graphed in order to minimize the use of resets. This will make it easier for you to compare your rates from baseline and self-control.

For additional practice construct a chart like the one shown in this chapter using the data you have been recording. Then construct a cumulative graph and plot these data according to the principles that have just been presented in this chapter.

---

If you answered Frame 12 correctly, then you understand cumulative graphs, and can go on to Chapter 6. If you missed any part of it (except for the addition) then do Frames 13 through 24.

**Review of Cumulative Graphs**

**13** Here's Clancy's data again:

|       | Number of Pages Read | Cumulative Number of Pages Read |
|-------|----------------------|-------------------------------|
| Day 1 | 10                   | 10                            |
| Day 2 | 20                   | _____                         |
| Day 3 | 15                   | _____                         |
| Day 4 | 0                    | _____                         |
| Day 5 | 15                   | _____                         |
| Day 6 | 20                   | _____                         |

|  | Number of Pages Read | Cumulative Number of Pages Read |
|---|---|---|
| Day 7 | 20 | ___ |
| Day 8 | 10 | ___ |

The first step in making a cumulative graph is to add each day's data to the total from the previous day. On Day 1, Clancy read 10 pages, and since he had a total of 0 prior to that (that is, no data kept) we add 10 and 0, and put this as the first number under **Cumulative Number of Pages Read**.

A. On day 2, Clancy read 20 pages. When we add this to the total from the previous day, we add 20 + ___ = ___.
B. On Day 3, he read 15 pages. We add 15 + ___ = ___.
C. On Day 4, he read 0 pages. We add ___ + ___ = ___.
D. Complete the chart.

A. 20 + 10 = 30

B. 15 + 30 = 45

C. 0 + 45 = 45

D.

|  | Number of Pages Read | Cumulative Number of Pages Read |
|---|---|---|
| Day 1 | 10 | 10 |
| Day 2 | 20 | 30 |
| Day 3 | 15 | 45 |
| Day 4 | 0 | 45 |
| Day 5 | 15 | 60 |
| Day 6 | 20 | 80 |
| Day 7 | 20 | 100 |
| Day 8 | 10 | 110 |

**14** Now go through the same steps with the following data on the

Cumulative Graphs

number of times that Betty Foldstein thanked her son when he helped her. Day 1: 2; Day 2: 5; Day 3: 3; Day 4: 6; Day 5: 2; Day 6: 2; Day 7: 5.

A. Set up your chart.

|       | Number of Thank You's | Cumulative Number of Thank You's |
|-------|-----------------------|----------------------------------|
| Day 1 | 2                     | 2 (0+2) (no previous data)       |
| Day 2 | 5                     | 7 (2+5)                          |
| Day 3 | 3                     | 10 (7+3)                         |
| Day 4 | 6                     | 16 (10+6)                        |
| Day 5 | 2                     | 18 (16+2)                        |
| Day 6 | 2                     | 20 (18+2)                        |
| Day 7 | 5                     | 25 (20+5)                        |

**15** A. Why is this kind of graph called a cumulative graph?

A. It's called a cumulative graph because you keep adding (or accumulating) each day's data to the previous total.

**16** A. What is a baseline and why should you obtain one?

A. A baseline is the rate of a response before you begin an intervention procedure. You would obtain a baseline in order to see if your self-control program or procedure was successful. That is, you would compare the rate of the response during baseline with the rate of the response after the self-control procedure has begun.

**17** Use Betty Foldstein's data to make the graph. On Day 1, Betty said, "Thank you", 2 times. Look at the graph below. Going across the bottom row is the Day. The first number you'll graph is for Day 1. Go across the bottom row until you read Day 1.

   A. The numbers going up the left side of the graph show the cumulative number of responses made. On Day 1, Betty made _____ responses, so you go up to line 2.
   B. The line marked Day 1 and the line marked 2 intersect or cross at a point. Make a dot at this point, and connect that dot to the 0 point (the lower left corner).

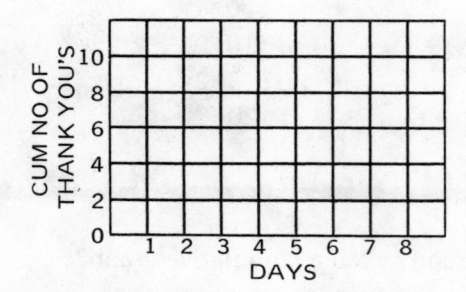

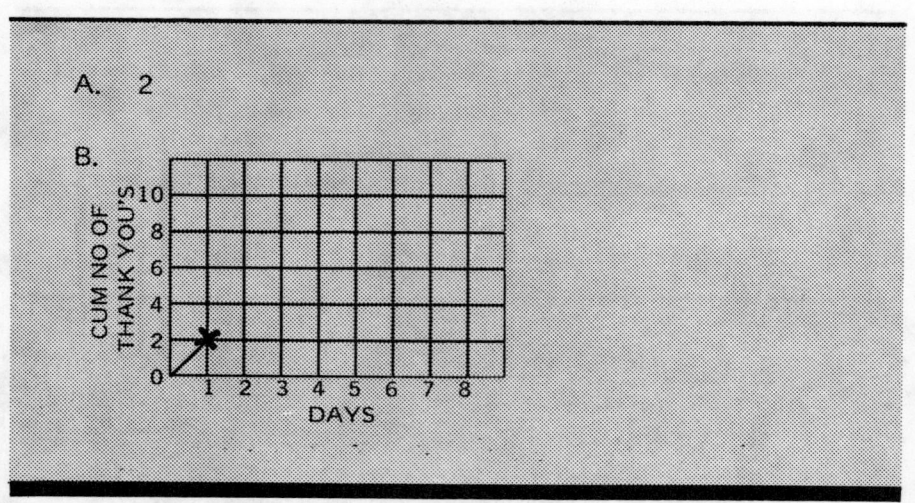

A. 2

B.

**18** A. On Day 2, Betty responded 5 times. To get our cumulative data we added _____ and _____ to get _____.

Cumulative Graphs

B. Plot this number (make a dot) at the place where the lines for this number of responses and Day 2 intersect. Connect this dot with the last one.

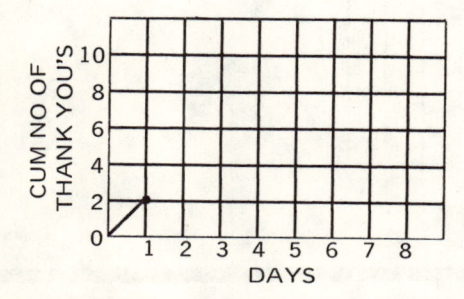

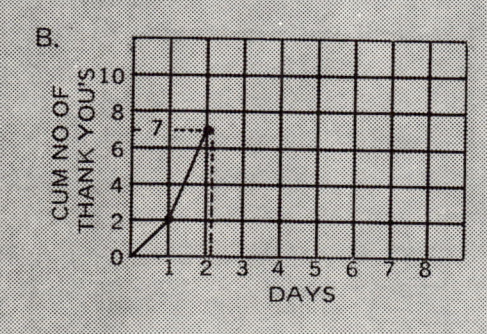

A. 2, 5, 7 (2+5=7)

B.

**19** A. On Day 3, Betty responded 3 times, which makes a total of 10. Plot this number.

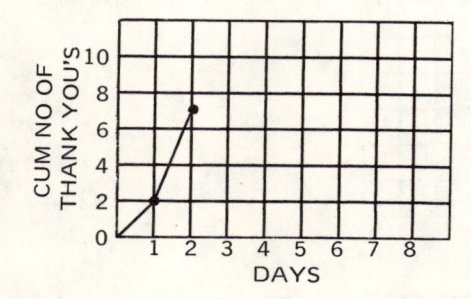

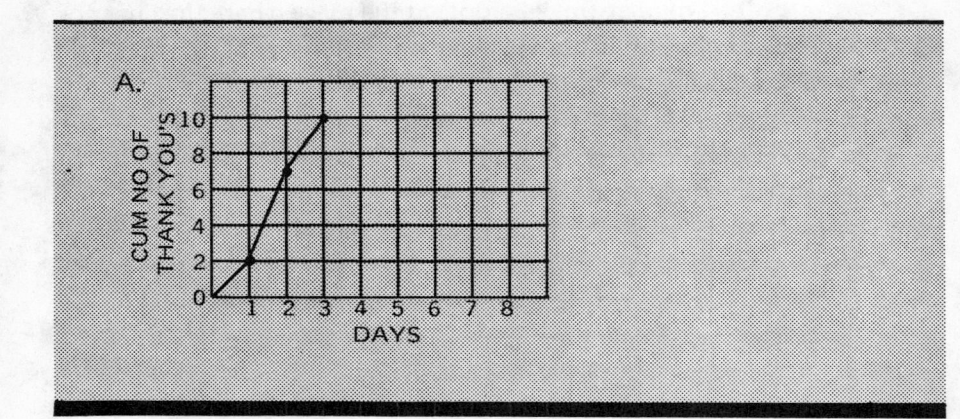

**20** As you can see in the above graph, Betty reached the top of her graph on Day 3. In order to continue graphing, we have to **reset** the graph. That is, we draw a line from the top of the graph to the bottom of the graph. (From Point A to Point B.)

A. Draw a reset.

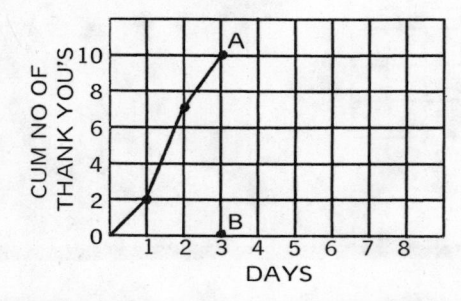

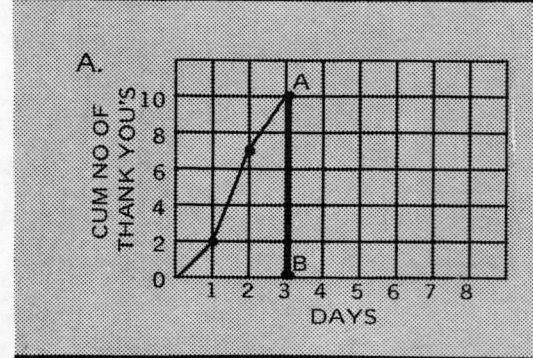

# Cumulative Graphs

**21** Now, we can record more of Betty's data. She already has a total of 10, so any data after the first reset will include this total of 10 plus whatever else is graphed.

    A.    On Day 4, Betty responded 6 times which gives her a cumulative total of _____.

    B.    Graph this data.

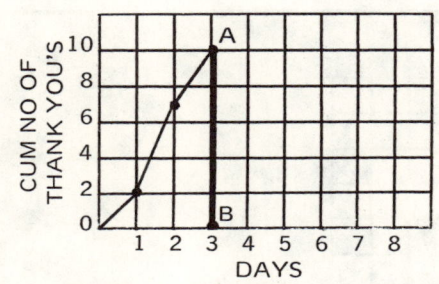

    C.    This point you just graphed indicates that Betty has responded a total of _____ times.

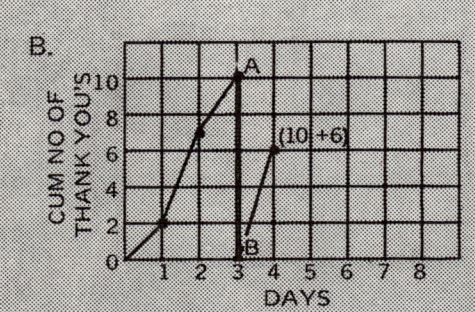

    A.  16

    B.

    C.  16

**22** A.    Graph the rest of Betty's data. (You will need one more reset.) See Frame 14 for the rest of the data.

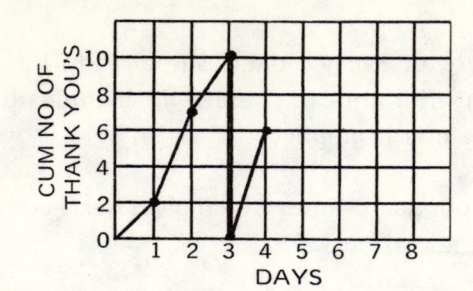

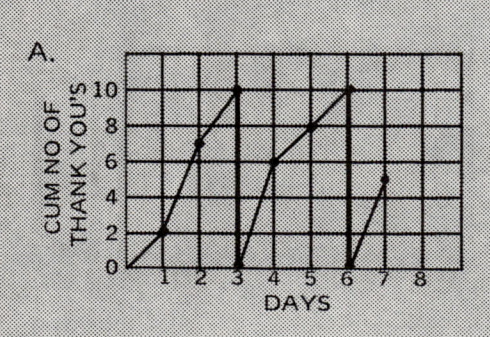

**23** A.  When do you use a reset?

A.  When you reach the top of the graph and there are more data.

**24** A.  Complete the following chart which contains the number of calculus problems that Joetta has done each day during baseline.

|  | Number of Problems | Cumulative Number of Problems |
|---|---|---|
| Day 1 | 10 | _____ |
| Day 2 | 15 | _____ |
| Day 3 | 15 | _____ |
| Day 4 | 20 | _____ |
| Day 5 | 15 | _____ |

Cumulative Graphs

|  | Number of Problems | Cumulative Number of Problems |
|---|---|---|
| Day 6 | 25 | _____ |
| Day 7 | 20 | _____ |
| Day 8 | 10 | _____ |

A.

|  | Number of Problems | Cumulative Number of Problems |
|---|---|---|
| Day 1 | 10 | 10 |
| Day 2 | 15 | 25 |
| Day 3 | 15 | 40 |
| Day 4 | 20 | 60 |
| Day 5 | 15 | 75 |
| Day 6 | 25 | 100 |
| Day 7 | 20 | 120 |
| Day 8 | 10 | 130 |

## 25
A. Plot the numbers from the above data.

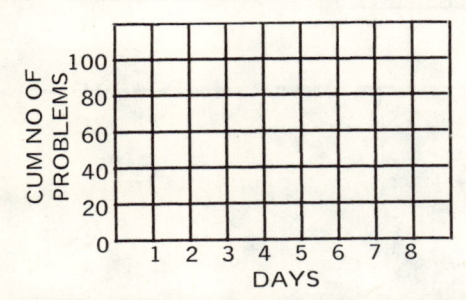

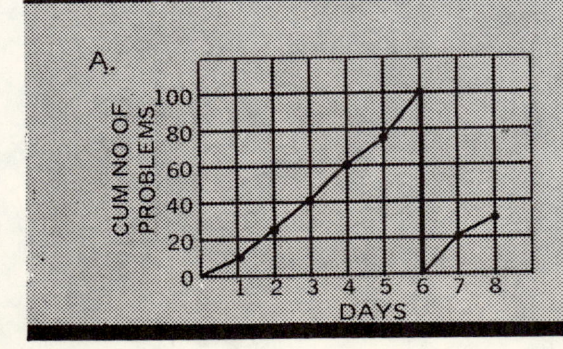

A.

**26** A. Why is this type of graph called a cumulative graph?

> A. Because you add (or accumulate) each day's data to the previous total and plot that number on your graph.

**27** Johnnie plants apple trees. His data for last week are: Day 1: 3 trees; Day 2: 4 trees; Day 3: 0 trees; Day 4: 2 trees; Day 5: 1 tree; Day 6: 4 trees; Day 7: 3 trees.

    A. Make a chart.
    B. Graph the data.

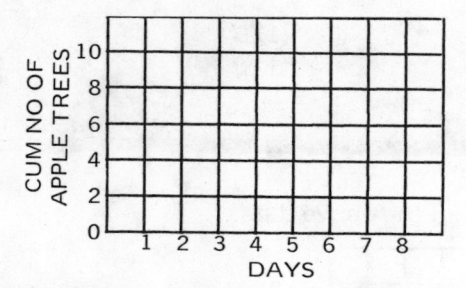

> A.
>
> | | Number of Apple Trees | Cumulative Number of Apple Trees |
> |---|---|---|
> | Day 1 | 3 | 3 |
> | Day 2 | 4 | 7 |
> | Day 3 | 0 | 7 |
> | Day 4 | 2 | 9 |
> | Day 5 | 1 | 10 |
> | Day 6 | 4 | 14 |
> | Day 7 | 3 | 17 |

## Cumulative Graphs

B.

[Graph: Cumulative No. of Apple Trees vs. Days]

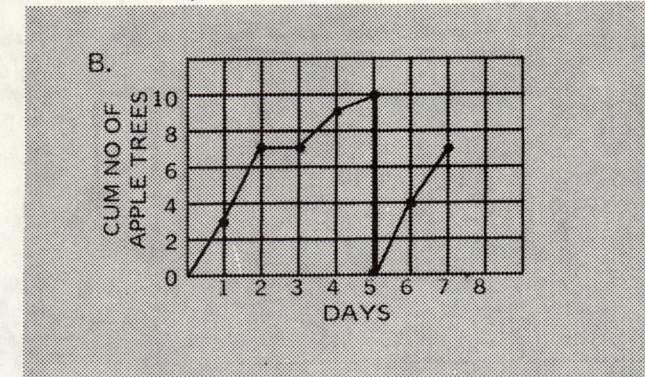

If you answered Frame 27 correctly, congratulate yourself, take a break if you wish, and then go on to Chapter 6. If you missed some part of this Frame, review this section.

# 6
## Setting Goals

**1** Let's use Betty Foldstein's data again. Her chart is below:

|  | Number of Thank You's | Cumulative Number of Thank You's |
|---|---|---|
| Day 1 | 2 | 2 |
| Day 2 | 5 | 7 |
| Day 3 | 3 | 10 |
| Day 4 | 6 | 16 |
| Day 5 | 2 | 18 |
| Day 6 | 2 | 20 |
| Day 7 | 5 | 25 |

Betty feels that one reason her son, Larry doesn't help her very often around the house is because she doesn't reinforce him when he helps. She has decided that showing her appreciation by saying, "thanks", may be enough of a positive reinforcer to increase her son's helping behavior. She also feels that she'd probably be more pleasant to live with if she began this project. Betty is ready to set a goal, but needs help in establishing what a realistic goal is.

The first step in setting a goal after establishing baseline, is to find the average rate from your baseline data. To find the average rate, divide the total number of responses by the number of days.

A. Fill in the following equation for Betty.

$$\text{Average rate} = \frac{\text{Total number of responses}}{\text{Number of days}} = \underline{\phantom{xxx}} = 3.57 \text{ (or about 4) responses per day.}$$

> A. $\dfrac{25 \text{ responses}}{7 \text{ days}}$

**2** A. What is the first step in setting a goal after baseline?

> A. Find the average rate from baseline.

**3** A. What is the average rate for Laura who ate a total of 15 chocolate bars in 3 days?
B. What is the average rate for Linda who made 30 posters in 5 days?

> A. $\dfrac{15}{3} = 5$ chocolate bars a day.
>
> B. $\dfrac{30}{5} = 6$ posters a day.

**4** A. What is the average rate for Paula who read for a total of 350 minutes over a seven-day period?

> A. $\dfrac{350 \text{ minutes}}{7 \text{ days}} = 50$ minutes a day.

Setting Goals

**5** A. After baseline, what is the first step in setting goals?

> A. Find the average rate from baseline.

**6** The second step in setting goals is to find the largest number of responses for any given period during the baseline. For general purposes we can assume that if the person performed the response this often, during baseline, then it is within his or her capacity. That is, the goal is not set too high.

A. Look back at Betty's data in Frame 1. What was her highest number of responses?

> A. Six responses (on Day 4).

**7** Jessica read her psychology last week and recorded the following baseline data: 30 pages the first day; 15 pages the second day; 35 pages the third day; 35 pages the fourth day; 0 pages the fifth day; 20 pages the sixth day; and 33 pages the seventh day.

A. What was her average rate during baseline?
B. What was the highest response rate for any given day?

> A. $\dfrac{168 \text{ pages}}{7 \text{ days}} = 24$ pages a day.
>
> B. 35 pages on the third (and fourth) day.

**8** A. What are the first two steps in setting a goal?

> A. 1. Find the average rate from baseline.
>
> 2. Find the highest number of responses for any given day, or period.

**9** Martin recorded baseline data on the number of statistics problems he did:

|  | Number of Problems | Cumulative Number of Problems |
|---|---|---|
| Day 1 | 10 | ___ |
| Day 2 | 12 | ___ |
| Day 3 | 13 | ___ |
| Day 4 | 8 | ___ |
| Day 5 | 17 | ___ |

A. Complete the chart.
B. Find the average rate during baseline.
C. What was his highest response rate?

> A.
>
> |  | Number of Problems | Cumulative Number of Problems |
> |---|---|---|
> | Day 1 | 10 | 10 |
> | Day 2 | 12 | 22 |
> | Day 3 | 13 | 35 |
> | Day 4 | 8 | 43 |
> | Day 5 | 17 | 60 |
>
> B. $\dfrac{60 \text{ problems}}{5 \text{ days}} = 12$ problems a day
>
> C. 17 problems on Day 5.

Setting Goals

**10** In order to set your goal follow the following rules:

1. To set a goal that will increase the rate of the response, set the goal **above** the average rate.
2. To set a goal that is within the individual's capacity, set the goal **equal to or below** his highest number of responses for any given day or period.

A. Use these principles to set a goal for Martin.

> A. His goal should be above 12 (his average rate) and equal to or below 17 (his highest rate). So you could have anyone of the following numbers: 13, 14, 15, 16, or 17.

**11** A. How can you set a goal that will increase the rate of an individual's response and be within his capacity?

> A. Set the goal above the average rate and equal to or below the highest response rate.

**12** Below is a graph showing Martin's baseline data. On the right side is a blank graph entitled **Self-Control**. On this side we will graph his goal line, which will be a **dotted** line. His data line (his actual performance after he begins his self-control procedure) will also be graphed there.

A. Graph his goal line, which will be 15 problems a day. (Remember to make your goal line cumulative.)

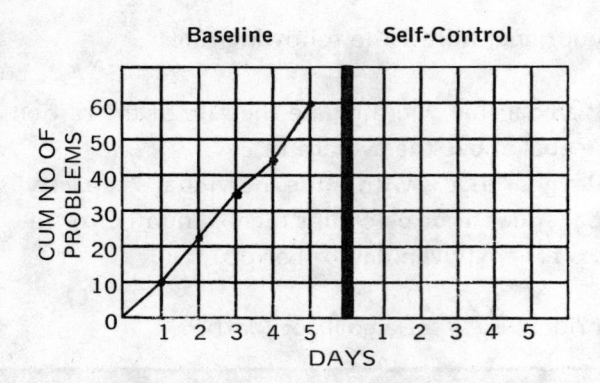

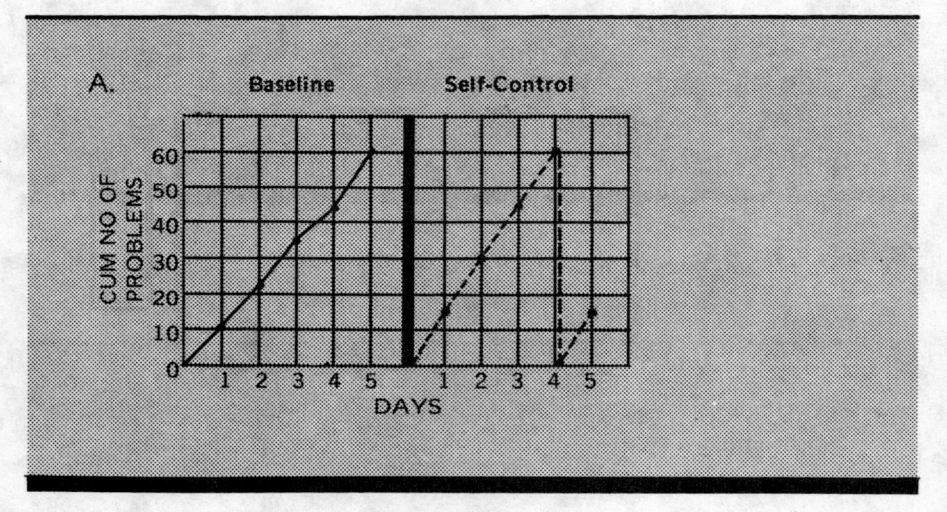

**13** During Martin's self-control program, he decides to drink a beer after he meets his goal of 15 problems a day. His data for the first week of the procedure phase is given below.

A. Complete the chart.

|  | Number of Problems | Cumulative Number of Problems |
|---|---|---|
| Day 1 | 15 | ____ |
| Day 2 | 25 | ____ |
| Day 3 | 20 | ____ |
| Day 4 | 15 | ____ |
| Day 5 | 20 | ____ |

Setting Goals

|  | Number of Problems | Cumulative Number of Problems |
|---|---|---|
| Day 6 | 25 | ____ |
| Day 7 | 20 | ____ |

B. Construct your own graph and plot the data. (Remember to draw your goal line.)
C. Was beer a positive reinforcer for Martin's doing problems?

---

A.

|  | Number of Problems | Cumulative Number of Problems |
|---|---|---|
| Day 1 | 15 | 15 |
| Day 2 | 25 | 40 |
| Day 3 | 20 | 60 |
| Day 4 | 15 | 75 |
| Day 5 | 20 | 95 |
| Day 6 | 25 | 120 |
| Day 7 | 20 | 140 |

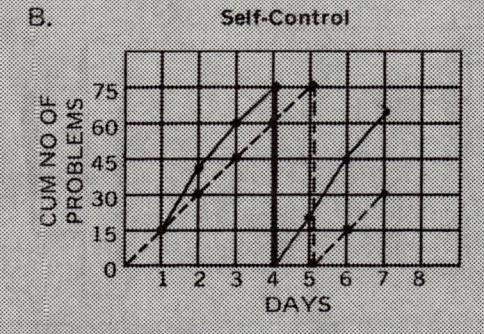

B. **Self-Control**

[Graph: CUM NO OF PROBLEMS (y-axis, 0 to 75) vs DAYS (x-axis, 1 to 8)]

C. Yes. He met his goal every day, and his rate increased to 20 pages per day when drinking beer followed doing statistics problems.

---

**14** Lulu works as a child psychologist in an institution. She feels that she spends too much time in the office, and not enough time interacting with the children. She took baseline data, and established a goal of 200 minutes a day with the children. (Her average rate was 180 and her highest response was 205.) She is going to have a 15-minute break whenever she reaches her goal. Her data for Week 1 of her self-control procedure are below.

A. Complete the chart.

|  | Number of Minutes With Children | Cumulative Number of Minutes With Children |
|---|---|---|
| Day 1 | 200 | _____ |
| Day 2 | 180 | _____ |
| Day 3 | 180 | _____ |
| Day 4 | 180 | _____ |
| Day 5 | 160 | _____ |

B. Plot the goal line as a dotted line and the self-control data as a solid line.

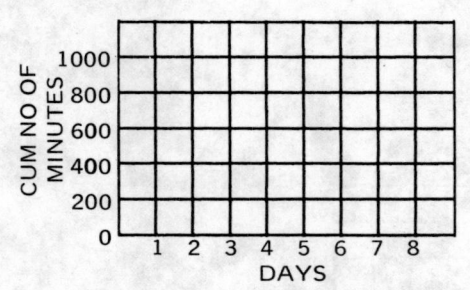

[Graph: CUM NO OF MINUTES (0–1000) vs DAYS (1–8)]

C. What was her average rate during the self-control procedure?
D. Did she ever get her 15-minute break?
E. Was the 15-minute break a positive reinforcer for her working with the children?

---

A.

|  | Number of Minutes With Children | Cumulative Number of Minutes With Children |
|---|---|---|
| Day 1 | 200 | 200 |
| Day 2 | 180 | 380 |
| Day 3 | 180 | 560 |
| Day 4 | 180 | 740 |
| Day 5 | 160 | 900 |

Setting Goals

B.

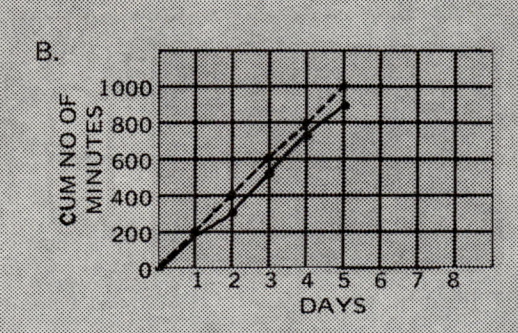

[graph showing cumulative number of minutes vs days, rising from 0 to ~900 over days 1-5]

C. 180 minutes a day.

D. Yes. (on Day 1)

E. No. Because it did not increase that rate of response, so it was not a positive reinforcer. (If you missed this, go back and review the definition of a positive reinforcer.)

**15** A. What steps do you go through in order to set a goal from your baseline data?

A. You find the average rate, then find the highest rate, and set the goal above the average rate but equal to or less than the highest rate.

**16** A. Set your goal from your data taken during the first part of this book. Choose a possible reinforcer; and beginning with Self-Test 2 see if you can increase your rate of answering frames. Fill in your data.

Average rate: _____ Highest rate: _____

Goal: _____    Possible positive reinforcer: _____

> A.    The answers are not provided for this frame.

**17** Stanley decides that he will mow lawns as a summer job. He arranges to save any money he makes up to $10.00 a day. If he makes more than $10.00, then he gets to spend it on whatever he wishes. He gets $2.50 per yard so he sets his goal at 5 yards per day. In other words, he'll have to meet his goal in order to have spending money.

A.  Complete the chart.

|       | Number of Lawns Mowed | Cumulative Number of Lawns Mowed |
|-------|-----------------------|----------------------------------|
| Day 1 | 4                     | ___                              |
| Day 2 | 2                     | ___                              |
| Day 3 | 3                     | ___                              |
| Day 4 | 2                     | ___                              |
| Day 5 | 0                     | ___                              |
| Day 6 | 2                     | ___                              |
| Day 7 | 1                     | ___                              |

B.  Graph the goal line and the self-control data.

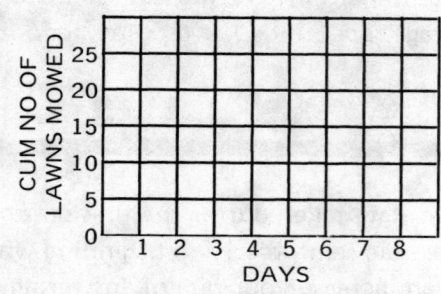

C.  What was Stanley's average rate?
D.  Did Stanley ever get to spend any money?

Setting Goals

A.
|       | Number of Lawns Mowed | Cumulative Number of Lawns Mowed |
|-------|-----------------------|----------------------------------|
| Day 1 | 4                     | 4                                |
| Day 2 | 2                     | 6                                |
| Day 3 | 3                     | 9                                |
| Day 4 | 2                     | 11                               |
| Day 5 | 0                     | 11                               |
| Day 6 | 2                     | 13                               |
| Day 7 | 1                     | 14                               |

B. [graph: CUM NO OF LAWNS MOWED vs DAYS]

C. $\dfrac{14 \text{ lawns}}{7 \text{ days}} = 2$ lawns per day

D. No.

**18** These last three results (Martin's, Lulu's, and Stanley's) represent three possible outcomes during self-control procedures.

1. Martin set up a goal within his capacity, selected an event to follow the response that **was** a positive reinforcer, and increased the rate of that response.
2. Lulu set up a goal within her capacity, selected an event that **was not** a positive reinforcer, and didn't increase the rate of the response.

3. Stanley set up a goal that **was not within** his capacity, and did not increase the rate of the response.
**Note:** Because the event (spending money) never followed the response, we do not **know** for sure whether the event was a positive reinforcer or not. In order to find out, you would have to lower the goal until it was met and have the event follow the response. If the rate of that response still does not increase then you can conclude that the event is not a positive reinforcer.

Look over these three situations, and their graphs, and indicate which of the following statements are true (T), and which are false (F).

A. If your goal is too high, then your self-control data line never meets your goal line.
B. If the selected event is not a positive reinforcer, then your self-control data line never meets your goal line.
C. If the selected event is a positive reinforcer, then your self-control data line never meets your goal line.
D. When the goal is set too high, you can't determine whether the event is a positive reinforcer.
E. If you meet your goal line at least once, and your rate doesn't increase, then the selected event is not a positive reinforcer.

A. T

B. F

C. F

D. T

# Setting Goals

> E. T

**19** A. What will happen if you set your goal too high?

> A. You will never meet your goal.

**20** A. What will happen if you have selected an event that is a positive reinforcer and set a goal that is within your capacity?

> A. The rate of the response will increase.

**21** A. What will happen if you set your goal within your capacity and have selected an event that is not a positive reinforcer?

> A. The event will follow the response at least once but your rate of responding will not increase.
> **Note:** If you were never able to meet your goal, then you should conclude that the goal was set too high.

**22** Look at the following graphs. Indicate which of the following situations has occurred.

1. The goal is set too high.
2. The event is not a positive reinforcer.
3. The goal is within capacity and the event is a positive reinforcer.

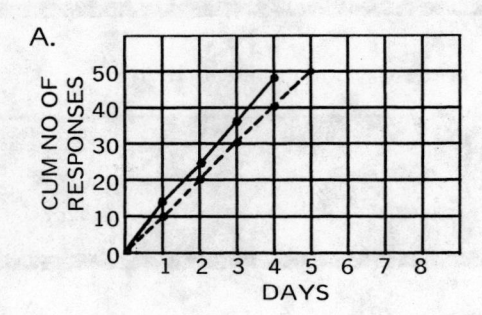

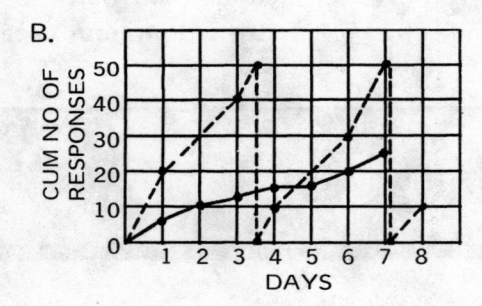

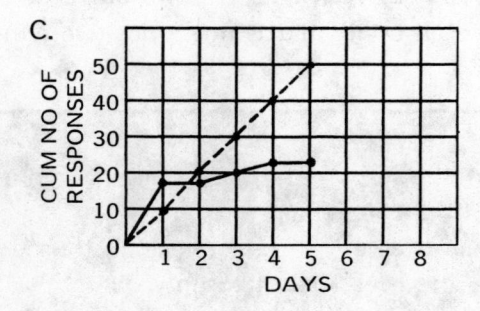

A.

B.

C.

Setting Goals

D.

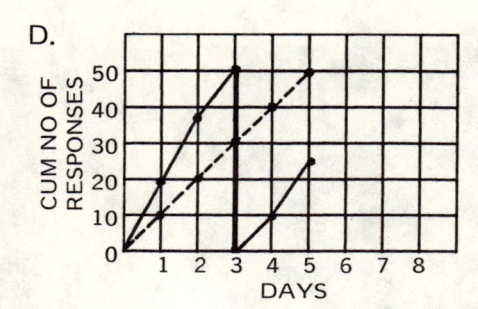

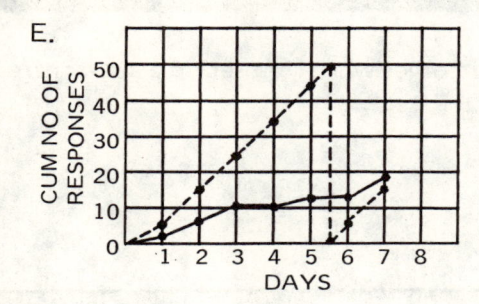

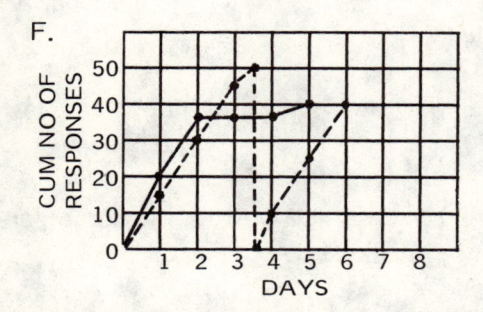

E.

F.

A. No. 3 (His self-control data line is consistently above his goal line.)

B. No. 1 (You don't know if the event is a positive reinforcer unless it follows the response. He never met his goal line.)

C. No. 2 (He met his goal line at least once, but his rate didn't increase.)

D. No. 3

E. No. 1

F. No. 2

**23** What are three possible outcomes when you set up a self-control program?

A.
B.
C.

A. The goal is set too high.

B. The goal is acceptable, but the event is not a positive reinforcer.

C. The goal is acceptable, the event is a positive reinforcer, and the rate of the response increases.

**24** If the goal is acceptable, and the event is a positive reinforcer, the rate of the response will increase. There is no need to change when this situation occurs. (Unless you want to make gradual increases in the goal.) In the other two situations, however, changes have to be made.

A. Look at A in the answer section of Frame 23. What recommendations would you make?
B. What recommendations would you make for the outcome as

Setting Goals

shown in answer B of the same frame.

> A. Lower the goal.
>
> B. Try a new event as a positive reinforcer.

**25** Bert is trying to increase his rate of reading job-related material. He has set a goal of 25 pages per night, and is planning to read **Saturday Review** as the positive reinforcer for reading job-related material. His graph for the first five days is below:

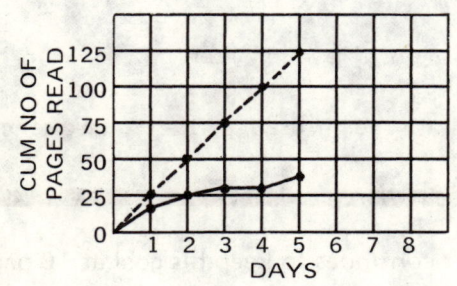

A. Which of the three situations has occurred?
B. What is your recommendation?

> A. The goal is too high.
>
> B. Lower the goal. You can use the current data for setting the new goal.

**26** Bert lowers his goal to 10 pages a night. (His average rate for the last five days was 8 pages a night and his highest response was 13 pages.) His data for the next five days are below:

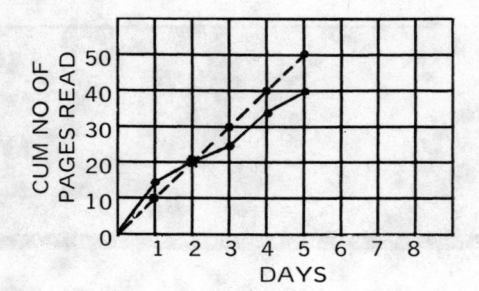

A. Which of the three situations has occurred?
B. What is your recommendation?

> A. The event was not a positive reinforcer.
>
> B. Change the event that's being used as the consequence.

**27** For his third attempt Bert continues to keep his goal at 10 pages a day, and decides to read **Playboy** for a given amount of time instead of **Saturday Review** when he reaches his goal. His data are given below:

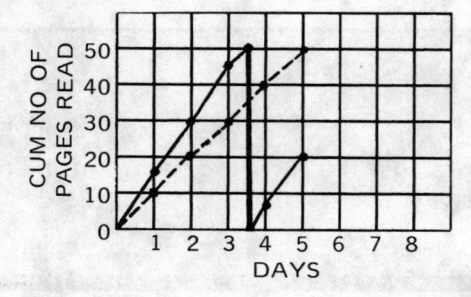

A. Which of the three situations has occurred?
B. What is your recommendation?

Setting Goals

> A. The goal is acceptable and the event is a positive reinforcer.
>
> B. Continue the program (or raise the goal).

**28** A. What are the two steps in establishing a goal?

> A. 1. Find the average rate from baseline. (The goal should be larger.)
>
> 2. Find the highest number of responses for any given period. (The goal should be equal to or less than the highest response rate — preferrably less than because it is reinforcing to succeed and the goal can always be increased.)

**29** A. How do you know if you have set a goal too high?

> A. You will never emit the response at a high enough rate to be reinforced. (Your self-control data line will remain below your goal line.)

**30** A. How do you know if the event you have selected is not a positive reinforcer?

> A. After the event follows the response at least once, and the rate of that response does not increase, you can conclude that the event is not a reinforcer. (i.e., you will meet your goal line at least once but the rate of that response will not increase).

**31** A. How do you know if your goal is set correctly, whether or not you have selected an event that is a positive reinforcer?

> A. The rate of that response will increase.

In setting goals you will want to do two things. First, decide which behavior you want to change. Second, set a terminal goal for that behavior. The first point is, for the most part, outside the scope of this text. I feel that it is up to **you** to decide (with possible suggestions from those affected by your behavior) which of your behaviors ought to be changed. (There are some exceptions, of course. For example, parents almost universally set goals for their children, and schools set goals for their students.) However, every individual responds in some ways which he or she would prefer to have occur at either a higher or a lower rate. (What was your New Year's Resolution?) Some of these are extremely important to interpersonal relationships, like the proportion of time you spend expressing your opinions as opposed to listening to someone else's views. Other specific behaviors are important for maintaining jobs, school work, social responsibility, etc. Still others are relatively unimportant (e.g., biting nails) but are of interest to the individual.

In this chapter we have focused mainly on point two, setting a terminal goal for your behavior. Once you have established that you want to change the rate of some response, how much of a change should be required before reinforcement is given? How great an increase or decrease should you expect? If your goal is set too high, you won't meet it, the response will fail to be reinforced, and as we all know by now, your response will extinguish. Or worse, you might go ahead, and "take your reinforcement" anyway, and the response of "failing" to meet your goal will be reinforced. When and if this occurs, you should arrange for someone else to control the reinforcer. That is, have another individual provide the reinforcement only after you have emitted the appropriate response. If you set your goal too low, then the chances of increasing the rate of that response will be greatly reduced.

# Setting Goals

Remember, in setting goals you will experience much more success in your program if you set a goal that is easily reached initially. Then, increase the criterion for reinforcement gradually in small steps until a desirable response rate is reached. After you have chosen a behavior to be changed, select a possible reinforcer, take baseline data, conduct a self-control procedure, and evaluate the data from that program.

Complete Self-Test 2 before going on to Section 3. Using the reinforcer you have selected, try to increase the number of correctly completed frames or the length of time per session you spend working on this book. Then take the information from Frame 16 of this chapter, plot your goal line on the graph you have constructed, and then plot your data for the rest of the book against this goal line, using the data you are recording.

---

In order to evaluate whether or not you have acquired the critical skills from the last three chapters, take the Self-Test on the next page. If you make any mistakes, review the appropriate chapter before proceeding to Section 3.

## SECTION 2

## SELF-TEST

**Count each of these questions as one frame for your data.**

**1** What is baseline?

**2** Why should you get a baseline?

**3** Make a chart and a cumulative graph for the following data on Clyde's rate of complimenting his daughter: 2 compliments on the first day; 3 on the second; 0 the third; 2 the fourth; 4 the fifth; 1 the sixth; and 2 the seventh.

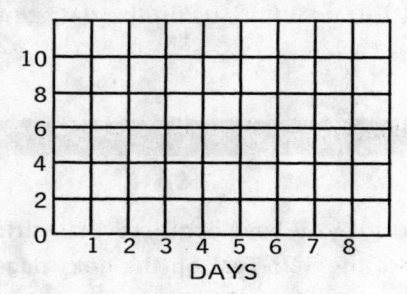

**4** Set a goal for Clyde.

**5** What are three possible outcomes of a self-control program?

**6** Which of the three outcomes occurs in each of these graphs:

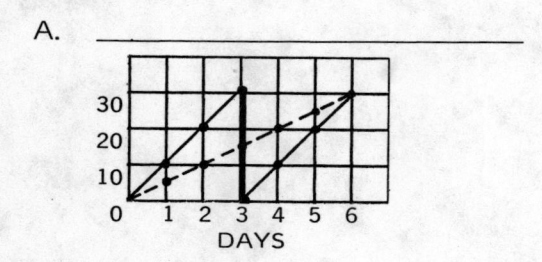

A. _____

B. _____

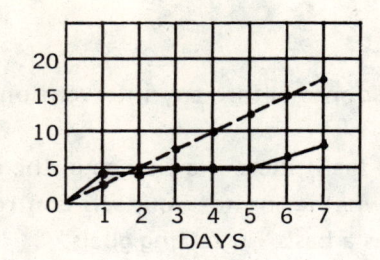

Self-Test

```
   20
   15
   10
    5
    0
      1 2 3 4 5 6 7
         DAYS
```

C  C. _____

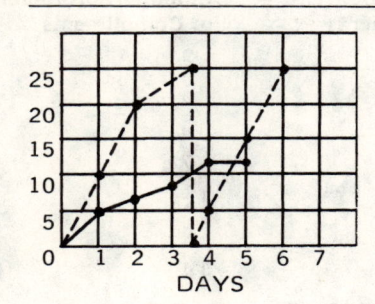

```
   25
   20
   15
   10
    5
    0
      1 2 3 4 5 6 7
         DAYS
```

D. _____

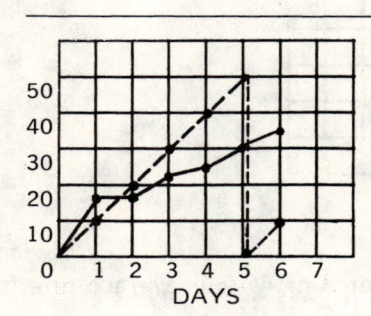

```
   50
   40
   30
   20
   10
    0
      1 2 3 4 5 6 7
         DAYS
```

Measuring Behavior Change

## ANSWERS

**1** Baseline is the rate of a response before any intervention is begun.

**2** You should get a baseline to see if there is a change in the rate of a response, and to determine whether or not your self-control procedure is effective. For use as a basis for setting goals.

**3**

|       | Number of Compliments | Cumulative Number of Compliments |
|-------|-----------------------|----------------------------------|
| Day 1 | 2 | 2 |
| Day 2 | 3 | 5 |
| Day 3 | 0 | 5 |
| Day 4 | 2 | 7 |
| Day 5 | 4 | 11 |
| Day 6 | 1 | 12 |
| Day 7 | 2 | 14 |

**4** Clyde's goal should be either 3 or 4. (His average rate is 2 and his highest response was 4.)

**5** The three possible outcomes are:

1. The goal is set too high.
2. The goal is correct, but the event is not a positive reinforcer.
3. The goal is correct, the event is a positive reinforcer, and the rate increases.

Self-Test 93

**6** A. The rate increased; goal is okay, and the event is a positive reinforcer.
B. The rate did not increase; the goal is okay, but the event is not a positive reinforcer.
C. The rate did not increase; the goal is set too high.
D. The rate did not increase; the goal is okay, but the event is not a positive reinforcer.

If you missed any of these, review the appropriate chapter. If you answered them all correctly, proceed to Chapter 7. Take a break if you wish to.

# Section 3

# Maintaining Behavior Change

In the last section you learned how to keep track of response rates under both baseline and self-control conditions, how to graph these data, how to set goals, and how to read and interpret graphs. Now you can measure and change response rates. However, there are other factors to consider in dealing with a self-control program. This last section will cover two areas that may affect your program once you have established it. One area involves the effect of other consequences on your behavior. The other deals with maintaining your target behavior.

If you want to increase the number of knitting stitches you make while visiting with your neighbor, you can easily set up a self-control program for this. But, if your wife is annoyed with this behavior, and yells, "Gerald, put away your knitting," you may find that your rate of knitting does not increase, even though your goal is set accurately, and you have already demonstrated that the event you are using is a reinforcer. There are other consequences (e.g., the punishment when your wife yells at you) that affect the rate of the response. In this section you'll learn how to recognize and deal with these consequences. Section 3 will also demonstrate how you can arrange for a response to be maintained, without having to conduct a formal program indefinitely.

The instructional goals of this section are:

- Chapter 7: When you have finished this chapter you will be able to recognize and deal with the concepts of extinction and punishment, and their effect on your self-control program.
- Chapter 8: When you have finished this chapter you will be able to identify and use procedures for maintaining the behavior that has been changed by a self-control procedure.

# 7
Integrating Extinction and Punishment into Self-Control Programs

**1** Ms. Rosevelvet is an excellent statistician. Because there are more men than women in her area of expertise she works very hard at maintaining her image as a competent statistician. However, every time there is a meeting, Ms. Rosevelvet is asked to take the notes at the meeting since she is the only woman present. During the last five weeks, she has attended two meetings a day. Sometimes she has declined to take notes. The data for her rate of declining for these five weeks are:

|        | Number of Refusals |
|--------|--------------------|
| Week 1 | 1 |
| Week 2 | 0 |
| Week 3 | 2 |
| Week 4 | 1 |
| Week 5 | 1 |

A. What goal should Ms. Rosevelvet set for herself if she wants to increase her rate of declining?

A. She should set a goal of two refusals a week.

**2** Starting with the sixth week Ms. Rosevelvet uses playing tennis on Saturdays as the reinforcer for having declined twice during the week. Here are the data for Weeks 6 through 8:

|        | Number of Refusals |
|--------|--------------------|
| Week 6 | 2 |
| Week 7 | 3 |
| Week 8 | 3 |

A. Is her procedure working?
B. Do you have any recommendation for Ms. Rosevelvet?

> A. Yes.
>
> B. You could recommend that she increase her goal, otherwise she's doing fine.

**3** It rained all weekend during the ninth week of her program. The tenth and eleventh weeks, her tennis partner was in the Bahamas, so she didn't play. Here are the data:

| | Number of Refusals |
|---|---|
| Week 9 | 3 |
| Week 10 | 2 |
| Week 11 | 0 |

A. Is Ms. Rosevelvet's program still successful?
B. What is happening to cause the change in her data?

> A. No.
>
> B. Her behavior of declining to take notes is not being reinforced. The behavior is undergoing extinction.

**4** A. What recommendations do you have for Ms. Rosevelvet?

> A. Ms. Rosevelvet should find another reinforcer, or make tennis more readily available. (For instance, have several possible partners, and find an indoor court.)

Integrating Extinction and Punishment

**5** Ms. Rosevelvet decided to use watching Saturday morning cartoons for the reinforcer if playing tennis was not possible. (It rained on Saturday during Week 12.) Her data during the next two weeks were:

|  | Number of Refusals |
|---|---|
| Week 12 | 4 |
| Week 13 | 5 |

A. Was her solution successful?
B. She decided to change her goal to 5 refusals per week. Was this reasonable?

A. Yes.

B. Yes.

**6** Mr. Hardnose attended all the meetings with Ms. Rosevelvet, and he got stuck taking notes whenever she declined. After Week 13, it seemed to him that he was taking notes more and more frequently. He greatly disliked taking notes, so whenever Ms. Rosevelvet declined, he muttered something about, "... pushy broads should know their place..." Ms. Rosevelvet's rate of declining for the next two weeks was:

|  | Number of Refusals |
|---|---|
| Week 14 | 7 |
| Week 15 | 8 |

A. What effect would you say that Mr. Hardnose's comment has on the rate of her declining?

A. It looks as though his comments are a definite reinforcer, although this may be the effect of the increased goal and the reinforcers of cartoons and tennis.

**7** Mr. Hardnose was on jury duty during the next three weeks and Mr. Crystal was given the responsibility of taking notes. Instead of muttering, Mr. Crystal went to Ms. Rosevelvet after every meeting during which he took notes and spent two hours with her trying to organize and write those notes. Her rate of refusal during those weeks was:

|  | Number of Refusals |
|---|---|
| Week 16 | 5 |
| Week 17 | 2 |
| Week 18 | 1 |

A. Ms. Rosevelvet is still using cartoons and tennis as the reinforcers when she meets her goal. Is the program working?

B. How would you explain this?

---

A. No.

B. It was probably more trouble to work with Mr. Crystal when he took notes than to do it herself. The consequences of declining were more unpleasant than taking notes.

---

**8** Here is a graph of Ms. Rosevelvet's refusal rate:

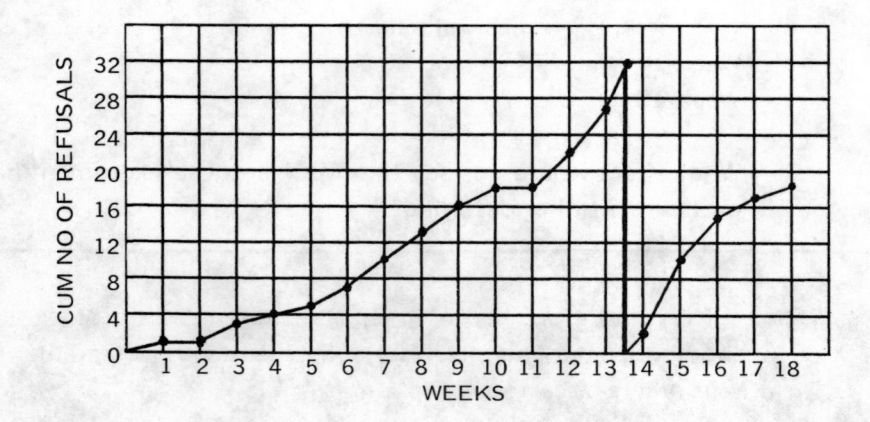

Integrating Extinction and Punishment 101

The Third Behavioral Principle is: **Punishment.**
**Responses that are followed by a punisher will decrease in rate.**

A. During what week did the punishment procedure begin for Ms. Rosevelvet?

> A. Week 16. (Her rate decreases from about 8 during Week 15 to 5 during Week 16.)

**9** A. How are the processes of punishment and extinction similar?
B. How are the procedures of punishment and extinction different?

> A. Punishment and extinction both result in a decrease in the rate of the response.
>
> B. In punishment, a response is followed by some event. In extinction, no specific event follows the response.

**10** Punishment occurs when a response is (A) _____ by an event and the rate of that response (B) _____.

> A. Followed
>
> B. Decreases

**11** A. How can you tell if a response is being punished?

B. How can you tell if a response is being extinguished?

> A. A response is being punished if it is followed by a stimulus or an event and the rate of that response decreases.
>
> B. A response is being extinguished if it has previously been followed by a positive reinforcer which no longer follows that response and the rate of that response decreases.

**12** Solomen is using a self-control program to increase his rate of working with his dog on an obedience training course. The reinforcer is the opportunity to make new music rolls for his player piano. (For every 15 minutes he works with his dog, he is allowed to do 50 bars of music.) On the fifth day he runs out of blank piano rolls.

A. What predictions can you make about his rate of working with his dog? (Assume that he makes no changes in his program. He waits for the piano rolls to come in.)
B. What is this process called?

> A. That rate will decrease.
>
> B. Extinction (the response is no longer followed by reinforcement).

**13** Sanchez was using banana ice cream to reinforce staying awake on his third-shift job. After 32 nights of banana ice cream, he thought he might switch to peach ice cream. His friend, George, convinced him that if he had used it successfully for this long, it must be an effective reinforcer. Sanchez's data for Days 28 through 35 are on the following page. (His goal is staying awake for the entire shift each night.)

Integrating Extinction and Punishment 103

|        | Awake |
|--------|-------|
| Day 28 | Yes   |
| Day 29 | Yes   |
| Day 30 | Yes   |
| Day 31 | Yes   |
| Day 32 | No    |
| Day 33 | Yes   |
| Day 34 | No    |
| Day 35 | No    |

A. Why is extinction occurring?

> A. Extinction is occurring because banana ice cream is no longer reinforcing Sanchez's staying awake behavior. Since that response is no longer followed by a positive reinforcer it is decreasing in rate (i.e., Sanchez is sick of banana ice cream).

**14** Penny is taking baseline data on the number of fencepost holes she digs each day. As she is digging them, her mother tells her to let her father do the job because it's not ladylike for her to do it. Here are Penny's data:

|       | Number of Post Holes |
|-------|----------------------|
| Day 1 | 10 |
| Day 2 | 12 |
| Day 3 | 14 |
| Day 4 | 14 |
| Day 5 | 18 |

A. What is happening to the rate?
B. What process is in effect?

> A. The rate is increasing.

> B. Reinforcement. It looks as if post-hole digging is being reinforced — either by her mother's attention, or possibly by keeping data. Seeing a response increase can sometimes be a very effective reinforcer. (In theory, Penny may be getting stronger and able to dig more post holes.)

**15** As a freshman in college Roger set up a self-control program to improve his study behavior. As the semester progressed his rate of studying increased to a point where he was studying so much that he saw his girl friend, Sarah Lou, only about two hours a week — a situation which bothered him greatly. He worried about the problem so much that he was unable to do very much studying, and as a result his grades also started to deteriorate.

A. What behavioral principle is in effect?

> A. Punishment. Roger's rate of studying was decreasing as a result of the introduction of an aversive situation (a punisher). Studying was followed by anxiety and the absence of Sarah Lou.

**16** Roger realized that his self-control program needed revision, so he agreed to spend time with Sarah Lou each night that he completed an adequate amount of studying for that day. He reset his goals on the basis of the previous week's data to ensure success with the program.

A. How did Roger deal with the punishment which was interferring with his self-control program?

# Integrating Extinction and Punishment

> A. Roger removed the punishing situation — he now gets to see Sarah Lou.

**17** A. What is the punishment principle?

> A. Responses that are followed by a punisher will decrease in rate.

**18** For the last five weeks, Samuel has had a program for increasing his rate of reading novels for literature class. He has reinforced his reading with a cup of cocoa for every 50 pages he reads. His rate of reading for the last week was:

|           | Number of Pages Read |
|-----------|----------------------|
| Monday    | 55                   |
| Tuesday   | 75                   |
| Wednesday | 50                   |
| Thursday  | 30                   |
| Friday    | 10                   |
| Saturday  | 0                    |
| Sunday    | 10                   |

Thursday Samuel began a new novel. He knows cocoa is still a reinforcer because he is using it to successfully maintain doing calculus problems.

A. What effect would you say the new novel has on Samuel's reading rate?
B. What is this process called?

> A. It is decreasing the rate.
>
> B. Punishment. The rate is decreasing due to the ongoing punishing effects of reading that novel.

**19** Samuel realizes that he has to read the novel to get through his literature class this semester, but he isn't quite sure how to do it. His friend, Ralph, figures that the cocoa is just not an effective reinforcer for that particular task.

    A. What would you suggest to increase the rate of Samuel's reading again?

> A. Try out some other reinforcers. Note: In some cases you may be able to eliminate the punishment. However, in this case it's not possible since he has to read the novel.

**20** A. How will Samuel know if this approach is successful?

> A. His response rate will increase again.

**21** A. How can you tell if extinction is occurring once a self-control program has begun?
    B. What can you do if extinction is occurring?
    C. How can you tell if punishment is occurring once a self-control program has begun?
    D. What can you do if punishment is occurring?

Integrating Extinction and Punishment                                    107

> A. The rate of the response will decrease if there are no changes in the program, or if the reinforcement is no longer available. (The rate of a response decreases when a response which has been previously followed by a reinforcer is no longer followed by a reinforcer.)
>
> B. You can try a new reinforcer.
>
> C. Punishment is occurring if the rate of the response decreases when some new object or event follows the response.
>
> D. You can eliminate the punishment and/or try to find a more powerful reinforcer.

You have seen how other factors can adversely affect your self-control program. However, you are now capable of analyzing those factors, seeing how they affect your program, and doing something to control the situation. You should be able to recognize when extinction or punishment procedures in self-control programs are occurring by examining the situation and looking at the data. If punishment is occurring, you can regain control over your behavior by eliminating the punisher. If extinction is occurring, you can add a more effective reinforcer.

Many individuals have successfully used punishment procedures in their self-control programs by arranging for a punisher to follow the response they wish to decrease. For instance, if you agreed to burn a ten-dollar bill every time you failed to do the dishes before going to bed, your rate of leaving the dishes unwashed all night would probably decrease. (I know mine would.)

These procedures may be used either alone or with a procedure providing positive consequences for desired behavior. However, they frequently require the cooperation of another individual to see that you either present or withhold the consequences you initially set up for a particular behavior. If you don't have another person involved, it is often easier or more reinforcing to drop the self-control program than to either do the dishes or follow through with the consequences.

A detailed discussion of the use of punishment procedures in self-control programs is beyond the scope of this book, but the bibliography will provide some recommended sources.

You have learned to recognize the need, set goals for, and implement a self-control program. The next and final question — How do I maintain my program once I have developed it? In Chapter 8 we will teach you some maintenance strategies to use once you have reached your goal. Is your rate of answering frames maintaining?

If you answered Frame 21 correctly, go on to Chapter 8. If you missed it, complete this review.

### Review of Extinction and Punishment

**22** A. Extinction is occurring when a response which has been followed by a positive reinforcer _____ _____.

B. This differs from punishment in that in punishment a response (which may also be followed by a positive reinforcer) is now followed by some new event and this results in _____ _____.

A. Is no longer followed by that reinforcer and the rate of that response decreases.

B. A decrease in the rate of that response.

# Integrating Extinction and Punishment

**23** Sunny washed her hair three times each week in the shower. She maintained this behavior by buying a new science fiction book every time she washed her hair. She moved to a new house with a smaller water heater. Every time she washed her hair, she ran out of hot water in the middle of her shower. After this, her rate of hair-washing decreased to an average of one and a half times per week even though she continued to buy a science fiction book whenever she washed her hair.

A. What process is occurring?
B. Justify your answer.

---

A. Punishment.

B. Punishment is occurring because the response rate decreased when it was followed by a new event, cold water (a punisher).

---

**24** Sunny had a larger water heater installed in her new house and her rate of hair-washing increased to three times a week. She continued reinforcing her hair-washing with science fiction books.

A. How did she deal with the punishment situation? (You may refer to Frame 21.)
B. Is positive reinforcement occurring now?

---

A. She eliminated the punishment.

B. Yes.

---

**25** Teresa was reinforcing letter-writing with a gallon of gasoline (for her car) for every letter she wrote to her many relatives. The last two weekends that she tried to buy gasoline for her car, she was unable to do so because of the gasoline shortage. So, she got out her bike, but for some reason, she didn't write any more letters to her relatives.

A. What was the reason?

> A. Her letter-writing was no longer being reinforced — it had extinguished.

**26** A. The rate of a response can be decreased during a self-control program through:

1.
2.

> A. 1. Extinction.
>
> 2. Punishment.

**27** A. How can you tell if punishment is occurring?
B. What can you do if it is?

> A. The rate of the response decreases when some new stimulus or event follows the response.
>
> B. You can find a stronger reinforcer or eliminate the punishment.

Integrating Extinction and Punishment

**28** A. How can you tell if extinction is occurring?
  B. What can you do if it is?

> A. The rate of the response decreases with no apparent change in the program — or when the reinforcement is no longer available.
>
> B. You can find a new reinforcer.

If you answered Frames 27 and 28 correctly, go on to Chapter 8. If not, review this last chapter.

# 8
# Establishing Maintenance Programs

**1**  Leonardo has been using a self-control program to increase the number of pages of journal articles that he reads. After seven weeks he has reached his goal of 25 pages per day. He is reinforcing his reading with watching two hours of television for every night that he reaches his goal.

He is quite satisfied with his progress, and decides that the behavior is well enough established to drop the program. So, he reads journal articles when he wants to and watches television when he wants to. After two weeks without the program he decides to see how well that behavior has been maintained. Although he doesn't remember specifically which days he read which articles, he does know which ones he has read during the last two weeks. He figures that his average rate of reading was 15 pages a day.

    A.    What is happening to the rate of his reading?
    B.    Which of the behavioral principles is in effect?

    A.    The rate of his reading is decreasing.

    B.    Extinction (Second Behavioral Principle).

**2**    A.    What can Leonardo do to increase his rate of reading to what it was before?

    A.    He can begin his program again. He can reinforce

reading journal articles.

**3** While it is useful to reinstate the program to its original form for awhile, in order to get the rate of the response back up to the desired level, you don't have to continue it indefinitely in full form. You have a few options for maintaining the behavior at a desirable rate without a highly structured program. One of these is keeping track of the rate of the response without using any other consequences.

A. How can you tell if graphing the behavior is an effective enough reinforcer to maintain the behavior at the desired rate?
B. What will happen if it is not?

A. If the rate of the response is maintained independently of other consequences then the graphing of the behavior is enough to maintain it at the desired level.

B. The rate of the response will decrease. It will extinguish.

**4** Leonardo graphs his reading rate for the next month, but uses no other consequence. His average rate is 27 pages per day.

A. Is graphing his response rate an effective reinforcer for Leonardo's journal reading?

A. Yes.

**5** A. How could you tell if graphing his response rate was no

# Establishing Maintenance Programs

longer an effective reinforcer for the reading behavior?

> A. His rate of reading would decrease even though he made no other changes in the program.

**6** A. What is one way that you can maintain a response without continuing a highly structured program?

> A. You can continue to graph the rate of the response but eliminate any other consequences.

**7** Valerie has been conducting a self-control program on her responses of telling her children how well-behaved they are when they are playing cooperatively. (She began this because she felt that the only time she paid attention to them was when they were misbehaving. If they were being "good", she, unfortunately, left them alone.)

She achieved a rate of 22 praises a day when she used knitting as the reinforcer for praising the children. She decided to graph her praising behavior as the only consequence, to see if it maintained her praising responses. That rate dropped to 16 a day, which she felt, was not sufficient.

A. What recommendations would you have for Valerie?

> A. She should use something in addition to graphing the behavior to reinforce praising.
> or
> She should reinstate the original program.

**8** Kaz has been using playing the pinball machine as a reinforcer for working in his garden. The pinball machine broke so he tried using graphing his behavior as the only reinforcer. The time he spent in the garden decreased from 90 minutes a day to 43 minutes a day.

   A. What process is in effect?

> A. Extinction.

**9** Kaz's friend, Max, talked with Kaz about this problem while they both looked over the graph. They did this each day for three days, and Kaz spent 50, 75, and 83 minutes working in the garden on those days.

   A. What effect did discussing his behavior with Max have on Kaz's gardening?
   B. What procedure is in effect?

> A. The time Kaz spent working in the garden increased.
>
> B. Positive reinforcement.

**10** Kaz thinks that Max's attention may be the reinforcer, so they arrange for Max to look at the graphs on a daily basis and comment favorably only if the amount of time spent working in the garden is 83 minutes or more a day. Max does not comment on the graph if the goal is not met.

   A. What will happen if Max's attention and comments are a reinforcer for Kaz's gardening?

# Establishing Maintenance Programs 117

> A. He will increase the rate he has set to at least 83 minutes a day.

**11** A. What, in addition to graphing your behavior, can be used to maintain the behavior after you stop your formal self-control procedures?

> A. Have a friend or your spouse check your graph and provide social consequences for your performance as reflected in the data. Social reinforcement is generally very effective in changing and/or maintaining behavior.

**12** Valerie started using knitting again as a positive reinforcer in her program, and the response rate went back up to 22 per day. She decided to try a new technique: if she keeps an average rate of 22 per day for an entire week, she and her husband will go dancing on Saturday night.

A. How will she know if this is an effective reinforcer?

> A. Her rate of paying attention to her children when they are playing cooperatively will stay at 22 a day or better.

**13** Some people begin self-control procedures using delayed reinforcers; for instance, reinforcing particular behaviors on a weekly basis.

A. How would they know if this kind of reinforcement

was effective for them?

B. What should they do if the delayed reinforcer is not effective?

> A. Their respective response rates will increase if it is effective.
>
> B. Try a more immediate reinforcer.

**14** What are three ways to maintain a response established by a self-control program?

A.
B.
C.

> A. Use graphing the response rate as the only consequence.
>
> B. Use a delayed reinforcer. Reinforce the maintenance of the appropriate rate every week or on a periodic basis.
>
> C. Have someone provide social consequences for your graphing.

**15** A. In each of the above situations how can you tell if the procedure was effective?

> A. The rate of the response will be maintained (or increased).

## Establishing Maintenance Programs

**16** A. How can you tell in each of the above cases if the procedure was not effective?

> A. The rate of the response will decrease.

**17** If you totally stopped any kind of intentional consequence (graphing, immediate, delayed, or social reinforcement) the response may be maintained simply by consequences that occur naturally in the environment.

A. How can you tell without taking daily data if the response is being maintained?

> A. Periodically take data and see if your rate is being maintained. (Every two months may be sufficient. With some types of behavior, however, a much shorter interval is desirable.)

**18** The basic rule for maintaining a response that was increased by a self-control program is to look at the data and see if your strategy is working. What are the four strategies given?

A.
B.
C.
D.

> A. Keep a graph of the rate of the response as the only consequence.
>
> B. Provide for social consequences for graphing the behavior.

C. Use a delayed reinforcer on a periodic basis.

D. Check the data intermittently (e.g., every two months) to see if the response rate is being maintained.

**19** A. How can you tell when a strategy is effective?

A. You can intermittently record and check the data to see if the behavior is being maintained.

This chapter has demonstrated methods of maintaining responses without using the elaborate systems typically required in the beginning of a program. Using long-range reinforcers, or simply graphing behavior can frequently maintain a response that has developed from a long, complex, self-control program. We have also seen that it is frequently useful to incorporate another individual into a self-control program to provide social consequences and to assist you in maintaining your program.

If you answered Frames 18 and 19 correctly, go on to the Self-Test for Section 3, which covers the entire book. If you missed some part, review this last chapter.

# SECTION 3

## SELF-TEST

**1** Define positive reinforcer.

**2** State the principle of extinction.

**3** How do you know if an event is a positive reinforcer?

**4** How can you guess what a positive reinforcer for an individual might be?

**5** Which of the events is being tested as a positive reinforcer in each of the following examples:

    A. Sweep the floor, then play cards.
    B. Play cards, then practice the piano.
    C. You smile at your husband, he smiles back.
    D. Take your medicine before you drink your milk.
    E. Drink milk before you take your medicine.

**6** Which of the following behaviors can be more readily observed and measured?

    A. Bowling.
    B. Biting your nails.
    C. Day dreaming.
    D. Caring about your kids.

**7**   A. Plot the following data on a cumulative graph:

|       | Number of Smiles Given |
|-------|------------------------|
| Day 1 | 34 |
| Day 2 | 26 |
| Day 3 | 30 |
| Day 4 | 27 |
| Day 5 | 33 |

```
     125
CUM NO OF
 SMILES  100
      75
      50
      25
       0
          1  2  3  4  5  6  7  8
                 DAYS
```

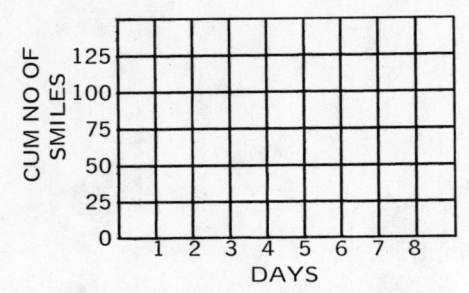

B. Set a goal using these data.
C. What was the average rate?
D. Draw a rough sketch of how the graph would look if the goal was too high.
E. Draw a rough sketch of how the graph would look if the event was not a positive reinforcer, but the goal was appropriate.
F. Draw a rough sketch of how the graph would look if the event was a positive reinforcer and the goal was appropriate.

**8** State the principle of punishment.

**9** How can you tell if a response that you are reinforcing is also being followed by a punisher?

**10** What can you do if this occurs?

**11** How can you tell if extinction is occurring in your self-control program?

**12** What can you do about it?

**13** Name four ways to maintain a response which has been increased to the desired level without continuing the entire self-control program.

**14** How can you tell if these procedures are working?

**15** What can you do if they are not working?

Self-Test 123

**16** What is baseline data?

**17** What characteristic gives the cumulative graph it's name?

**18** How are the procedures of punishment and extinction different? In what way are their processes alike?

# ANSWERS

**1** A positive reinforcer is an object or event that follows a response and increases the rate of that response.

**2** Responses which have been previously established or maintained by reinforcement will decrease in rate when that reinforcement is withheld.

**3** The two ways to know if an event is a positive reinforcer are:

1. Have the event follow some response and see if the rate of that response increases.
2. If the event has been following some response, stop presenting the event following that response and see if the rate of that response decreases.

**4** You can guess what a reinforcer for a person might be by watching how the individual spends his or her time. High rate responses are likely to be reinforcers.

**5**
A. Playing cards.
B. Practicing the piano.
C. Your husband smiling.
D. Drinking milk.
E. Taking medicine.

**6** A and B are more readily measurable and observable.

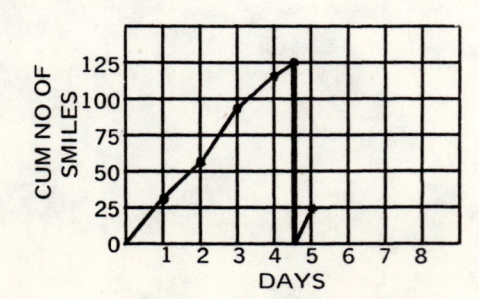

**7**

# Self-Test

B.  31, 32, 33, or 34 smiles per day.
C.  30 smiles per day.
D.

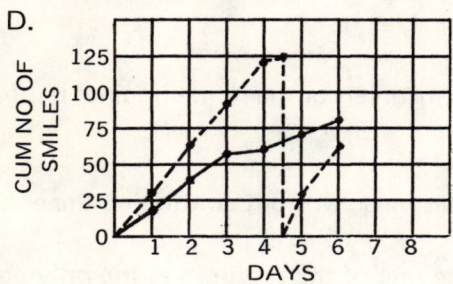

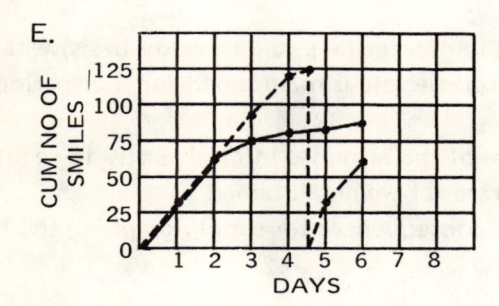

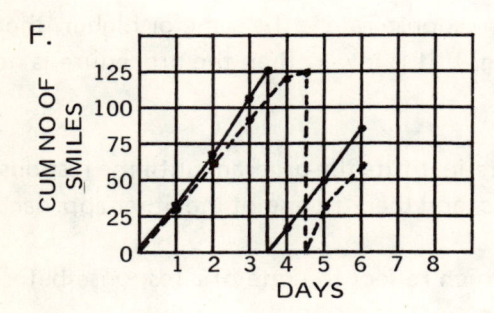

E.

F.

**8** Responses that are followed by a punisher will decrease in rate.

**9** If the response is followed by some new event (in addition to the positive reinforcer) and there is a decrease in the rate of that response, then the event is a punisher.

**10** You can either eliminate the punisher or obtain a stronger reinforcer.

**11** Extinction is occurring if the rate of the response begins to decrease with no other changes in the program or when the positive reinforcer is no longer available.

**12** You can obtain another reinforcer, or make the original reinforcer available.

**13** Four ways to maintain a response without continuing the entire self-control program are:
1. Use graphing the rate of the response as the only consequence.
2. Use a delayed reinforcer (e.g., on a weekly basis) when the desired response rate is maintained for that period of time.
3. Check the rate of the response intermittently to see if the response rate is being maintained.
4. Provide social consequences for simply graphing the behavior.

**14** Look at the data. If the response rate is the same or higher, then the procedure is working. If it is lower, then the procedure is not working.

**15** If they are not working, re-institute the program until the response rate is back to what it was, and then try one of the other approaches.

**16** Baseline data are data which reflect the rate of a response before any intervention is begun.

**17** The cumulative graph gets its name from the fact that you add (or accumulate) the current data to the previous total and plot that number.

**18** Punishment and extinction differ in that punishment is the presentation of a stimulus or an event (a punisher), and extinction is the termination or withholding of a stimulus or an event (a reinforcer). They are similar in process in that they both result in a decrease in response rate.

## Conclusion

Congratulations! You are ready to begin your own self-control program! You should now be able to identify, measure, and change behavior. You are equipped to evaluate this change, eliminate interferring consequences, and maintain certain behaviors. Many of the responses that you change may produce changes in your environment to the extent that the environment itself will maintain your new response. For instance, if you have conducted a self-control program to increase your rate of smiling, your smiling will probably increase the number of people who smile at you. This, in turn, may maintain a high rate of smiling. Or, if you have increased your rate of making comments in a class, classmates and the teacher may maintain this behavior by their attention and approval.

There is one more thing to remember when you're trying to establish an effective self-control program: Many people who institute programs generally pick out a behavior that presents a problem for them, one which they have great difficulty in controlling. Typical examples are smoking and overeating. These behaviors can be effectively controlled through the procedures we have learned, but the reader will find considerably more success in establishing and maintaining a self-control program of this nature **after** he or she has experienced success with less difficult problems. For example, reading performance, compliments to others, completing tasks on schedule, etc. are somewhat easier to begin with.

Behaviors such as smoking and overeating are not as easy to modify because both activities are highly reinforcing and have usually been occurring for a long period of time. Thus, these types of behaviors are very complex and require considerable expertise in self-control techniques. Trying to eliminate smoking behavior as your first self-control program would be like teaching an individual to do a one-and-a-half forward flip before he or she has learned to do a simple front head dive, or giving a first grader a college-level text to master.

Self-control, like many behaviors, is complex. It must be learned from the ground up. If you find yourself giving up a self-control program before reaching your behavioral goal, don't give up! Restructure the program, or begin with a simpler program and then work up to the more complex ones. Incidentally, if you stop a self-control program before you've met your goal and you don't earn the reinforcer, don't take that reinforcer! You may reinforce non-self-controlling behavior.

As part of this text, you have been keeping data and setting goals for your performance. How did you do? After completing Self-Test 3, plot that data and then look at your graph. Did you reach your goal line? If not try to determine why. Was the event you selected a reinforcer? Was your goal set too high?

Through the procedures and methods outlined in this book you now have the basic skills to modify and control your own behavior. Good luck, and remember: **THROUGH SELF-CONTROL ONE CAN TRULY ACHIEVE FREEDOM.**

**Instructions for Data Sheet**

This sample data sheet is a model for you to use when recording the data on your progress throughout this book. After you have constructed your own data sheet fill in the **Behavior of Interest** (the response that the self-control program is designed to modify). In this case the behavior of interest is "the number of frames that you complete correctly", or "increasing the total time you spend per session working in this book." These will include the frames in the review sections you are instructed to complete.

When you begin Chapter 1 fill in the line for Session 1 in the Data Record. Write in the date and the time that you start. When you stop, record that time. Also record the total amount of time that you've spent working on that session.

Next, record both the number of frames that you have completed and the number that you have completed correctly.

When you start working in the book again, even if it's the same day, start with the next line and complete it in the same manner. (Refer to the other portions of this data sheet when you reach the appropriate parts in the text.) Continue taking data in this manner until you finish **Developing Self-Control**.

Behavior of Interest _____.
Reinforcer _____.
Average Rate _____.
Highest Rate _____.
Goal 1: _____ Goal 2: _____.

## DATA RECORD

| Session | Date | Beginning Time | Ending Time | Elapsed Time | Frames Completed | Frames Correct |
|---------|------|----------------|-------------|--------------|------------------|----------------|
|         |      |                |             |              |                  |                |
|         |      |                |             |              |                  |                |
|         |      |                |             |              |                  |                |
|         |      |                |             |              |                  |                |
|         |      |                |             |              |                  |                |
|         |      |                |             |              |                  |                |
|         |      |                |             |              |                  |                |
|         |      |                |             |              |                  |                |
|         |      |                |             |              |                  |                |
|         |      |                |             |              |                  |                |

## CUMULATIVE CHART

| Session | Responses | Cumulative Responses |
|---------|-----------|----------------------|
|         |           |                      |
|         |           |                      |
|         |           |                      |
|         |           |                      |
|         |           |                      |
|         |           |                      |
|         |           |                      |
|         |           |                      |
|         |           |                      |
|         |           |                      |

## CUMULATIVE GRAPH

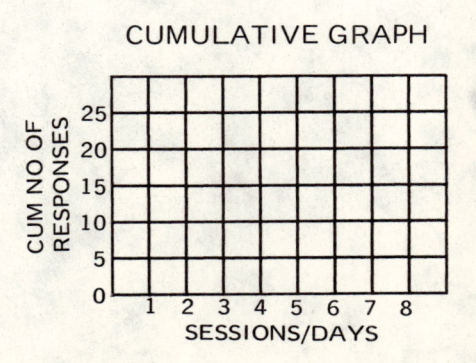

# Appendix

# BEHAVIORAL PRINCIPLES

### First Behavioral Principle: Positive Reinforcement

**Responses that are followed by a positive reinforcer will increase in rate.**
As a **procedure**: Positive reinforcement is the presentation of a reinforcing stimulus or event following a response.
As a **process**: Positive reinforcement is the increase in the probability or the rate of a response when that increase results from the presentation of a reinforcer.

### Second Behavioral Principle: Extinction

**Responses which have been previously established or maintained by reinforcement will decrease in rate when that reinforcement is withheld.**
As a **procedure**: Extinction is the withholding or termination of the reinforcement for a response which has been previously established or maintained through the use of that reinforcement.
As a **process**: Extinction is the decrease in the probability or rate of a response which results from the withholding or termination of the reinforcement for that response which was previously reinforced.

### Third Behavioral Principle: Punishment

**Responses that are followed by a punisher will decrease in rate.**
As a **procedure**: Punishment is the presentation of a punisher (an aversive stimulus or event) immediately following a response.
As a **process**: Punishment is the decrease in the probability or rate of a response which results from the presentation of a punisher.

# Bibliography

Ascher, M. and Cautela, J. R. "Covert negative reinforcement: An experimental test." **Journal or Behavior Therapy and Experimental Psychiatry,** 1972, 3, 1-5.

Bandura, A., Grusec, J. E., and Menlove, F. L. "Some social determinants of self-monitoring reinforcement systems." **Journal of Personality and Social Psychology,** 1967, 5, 449-455.

Barber, T. X., DiCara, L. V., Kamiya, J., Miller, N. E., Shapiro, D., and Stoyva, Johann (Eds.) **Biofeedback and Self-Control.** Chicago: Aldine-Atherton, 1971.

Budzynski, Thomas H., Stoyva, Johann M., Adler, Charles S., and Mulhaney, Daniel J. "EMG biofeedback and tension headache: A controlled-outcome study." Unpublished paper. University of Colorado Medical Center, Denver, Colorado.

Cautela, Joseph R. "Covert negative reinforcement." **Journal of Behavior Therapy and Experimental Psychiatry,** 1970, 1, 273-278.

Cautela, Joseph R. "Treatment of smoking by covert sensitization." **Psychological Report,** 1970, 26, 415-420.

Cautela, Joseph R. "Covert extinction." **Behavior Therapy,** 1971, 2, 192-200.

Ferster, Charles B., Nurnberger, John I., and Levitt, Eugene B. "The control of eating." **Journal of Mathetics,** 1962, 1, 87-109.

Goldiamond, Israel. "Self-control procedures in personal behavior problems." In R. Ulrich, T. Stachnik, and J. Mabry (Eds.) **Control of Human Behavior.** Glenview, Illinois: Scott, Foresman, 1966.

Kanfer Frederick H. "Self-Regulation: Research, issues, and speculations." In C. Neuringer and J. L. Michaels (Eds.) **Behavior Modification in Clinical Psychology,** New York: Appleton-Century-Crofts, 1970.

Kanfer, Frederick H. "The maintenance of behavior by self-generated stimuli and reinforcement." In A. Jacobs and L. B. Sachs (Eds.) **The Psychology of Private Events.** New York: Academic Press, 1971.

Kanfer, Frederick H. and Karoly, Paul. "Self-control: A behavioristic excursion into the lion's den." **Behavior Therapy,** 1972, 3, 398-416.

Kanfer, Frederick H. and Karoly, Paul, "Self-regulation and its clinical application: Some additional conceptualizations." In R. C. Johnson, R. R. Dokecki, and O. H. Mowrer, (Eds.) **Conscience, Contract and Social Reality: Theory, and Research in Behavioral Science.** New York: Holt, Rinehart and Winston, 1972.

Kazdin, A. E. "Response cost: The removal of conditioned reinforcers for therapeutic change." **Behavior Therapy,** 1972, 5, 293-309.

Lichtenstein, E. and Keutzer, C. S. "Experimental investigation of diverse techniques to modify smoking: A follow-up report." **Behaviour Research and Therapy,** 1969, 7, 139-140.

Mahoney, Michael J. "Research issues in self-management." **Behavior Therapy,** 1972, 3, 45-63.

Mahoney, M. J., Moura, N. G., and Wade, T. C., "The relative efficacy of self-regard, self-punishment, and self-monitoring techniques for weight loss." **Journal of Consulting and Clinical Psychology,** 1973, 40, 404-407.

Mahoney, Michael J., and Thoreson, Carl E. **Self-Control: Power to the Person.** Monterey, California: Brooks/Cole, 1974.

Bibliography

Premack, David. "Mechanisms of self-control." In W. Hunt (Ed.) **Learning Mechanisms in Smoking.** Chicago: Aldine Press, 1970.

Skinner, B. F. **Science and Human Behavior.** New York: Macmillan, 1953.

Thoreson, Carl E., and Mahoney, Michael J. **Behavioral Self-Control.** New York: Holt, Rinehart and Winston, Inc., 1974.

Watson, David L., and Tharp, Roland G. **Self-Directed Behavior: Self-Modification for Personal Adjustment.** Monterey, California: Brooks/Cole, 1972.

## Validation

The results of validation were obtained using 25 students as subjects. A pre- and posttest design was used for validation.

The average error rate was tabulated for both pre- and posttest scores. The rates were 77.8% and 6.5% respectively, while the average score was 22.2% on the pretest and 93.5% on the posttest. The average improvement rate was 71.3% **over** pretest scores.

In addition, 470 Introductory Psychology students who used the text were asked to evaluate it. When asked whether they enjoyed the reading, 74% responded yes; 93% said they felt that the reading was easy; 69% rated the material as interesting; 81% stated that the material was relevant; 85% of the students said they felt the principles were presented in a clear-cut manner; and 86% said that the examples presented helped them to understand the material.

Our objectives were to create a relevant and interesting book that would be easy to read and understand, while effectively teaching some of the basic principles of behavior modification. We believe that these objectives have been reached.